PRIDE OF AFRICA

MILTON C. KALWIHULA

Introduction

Dear African youth, as myself being one of the African youths living in Tanzania, busy looking for the right pillar around, as a supportive gear minimizing challenges from opportunities by being a manufacturer and fabricator of problems jeopardizing youth life path and with its side effects on different area that supports youth upgrowth strongerly, enegetically, and courageously in the job vacancies, potential businessmen and women e.t.c. I believe in using C^- resources with B^+ results. I am an active member of Tanzania's patriotism and the African continent at large.

I'm also recognizant of the former and current friends for personal character growth. I am so honoured and humbled to see great changes in youth. This book is a fine-tune of the disciplinary barrack life cautions because of numerous lifestyles it retouches for the purposes of personal growth from great to significance.   Touching   socio-cultural, economic landscapes and it is a life style multi-disciplinary book for all ranks of people.

Preface

The book's context is to clearly spot out the youths' life path through employment and public relation at the workplace and slightly identifying the social challenges following up the dream line-break. The book is also a layout on the business, psychological intents, economic, social, biographical, historical and tourist based issues. What this book uncovers is hopefully expected to spark light of interests, influence, hobbies and talents in your personality. It will help you discover the potentials that feature the content of your character. It will build your business platform, your career if its not yet discovered or its dead. This book will recover it. It also centralizes all life challenging factors and gives its solution, it shapes and strengthens every individual following particular dreams by inspiring customers, clients, employers, employees, friends and entrepreneurs. The book is a comforter to lonely persons, orphans, widows, divorced ones, ignored persons e.t.c. The book is also a job seaker's phychotherapists.

Editors:

St. Augustine University of Tanzania (SAUT)-Lecturer, Mr. Masanja

Road to Success Inspirational Talk Ltd C.E.O Mr. Rodrick Nabe

THE REASON THAT INSTIGATED ME TO WRITE THIS BOOK.

- Vivid observation of the youth being challenged in winning interviews.
- The African youths have challenges on how to make themselves fit for job vacancy's requirements
- The way talents and skills of Africans are deliberately not promoted.
- How Promotion and demotions are pursued/perceived.
- Cash flow and bankrupty at workplace.
- Entrepreneurship; softly procrastinated.
- Problems from individuals on how to build careers.
- How families, domiciles and clans contribute to the diminishing of youth's focus.
- Disquising deceiving best performer from the undeceiving perfomer.

CONTENTS

Acknowledgments

My special thanks are with God who has really supported this work unconditionally. Let my thanks also go to my wife Julieth Rugeiyamu, who firmly stood by me during the collection of pieces of information for this document. My child Mercy Milton who has been encouraging me through her words of wisdom harmony and joy. To all whom I once passed in their hands; in my hustles, up to this stage. Some are listed below:- my step mother Joyce Charles who was a blessing during my hard and sad time when I was young. My step father Pastory Magezi, from Kitwe village who collected his strengths for me to excel as I am today. My cousin Tadeus Mtarubukwa, for his hand to hand support of testifying my life focus from the scratch. Secondary school teachers Mr. & Mrs. Ndyetabula who created an environment for me to endure the harship in my school life. Steve Ogweyo's Family which really supported me in handling the street life and offered me spiritual encouragement. Bwiru secondary school teacher Mr. Micheal Rwezaula and his Familly who played a big role in strenthening my life standard and availling humanly life standards to avail humanly perspectives. They also strongly stood by me during my marriage accomplishments and continue to show parental love to me. Pastor Alex Kishimba, who gave me a room to expose my insights, Pastor Charles Mathew my spiritual father. The late pastor Deogratius who really played a role in shaping me spiritually and kindly supported my marriage undertakings. Pastor Majembe who built my capacities in God's doctrines and provided me with spiritual counselling, Mr Martin Modest, my best friend for numerous ideal accomplishments. My friends indeed, Mr. & Mrs Brithon Jonathan for their endless social, material, mental, financial support. Mr Paul Masatu for his economic contents and capacity building. Mr Japhet Makwaia for his financial management counselling. RUCCO staff, Scholastica Rwezaula for her multi-social assistance. My brother Nelson Christopher for his life capturing skills. The list of valuable individuals is endless. I pray that the mighty Lord rewards their fruitful efforts abundantly.

CHAPTER ONE

PRIDE OF AFRICA

The legacy of Africa:
Africa is the second largest continent in the world with 58 countries. Seven (7) of these countries are listed as Islands (Madagascar, Zanzibar, Comoro Island, Chief's-Botswana-Island, Mauritius, Seychelles and Mumbo Island). Africa is approximately said to have a population of about 1,125,307,147 people. Africans are proud of togetherness, peace, hospitality, nature and subordination. The African people share common cultural, interests as described in the integrated Xhosa-proverbs known by the name of *"Abantu, Omuntu, Ngumuntu, Ngabantu"*. These concepts interpret African people as people who invest their values and beliefs in the culture of oneness. Africa has many resources and many tourist attractions which are supposed to be turned into reality for the purpose creating people's daily needs and eventually making the World a better place to live. The fact of the matter is that the tourist attractions and natural resources which Africa embodies are plenty to the brim. Even if everybody in Africa would flag-light a single entity and decide to expose it to the rest of the World, the package of these resources and attractions won't be finished or get disseminated to reach all people around the world who want to know or hear about them. Africa is a rich continent with a good number of proactive and productive youths. I'm pleased to state the name **"AN ENDOWED PLACE OF THE WORLD"**; meaning that it is the gifted land as it entails the

best of the symbols of beauty, nature and power. It encompasses humble people with hospitality and good perceptions upon visitors from across the globe. Africa still recites the voices, and lives on the spirit of the honoured state founders such as Mwalimu Julius Kambarage Nyerere of Tanzania, Kwame Nkrumah of Ghana, Nelson Mandela of South Africa, Thomas Sankara of Burkina-Faso (Upper Volta) Jomo Kenyatta of Kenya, Samora Machel of Mozambique, Patrick Lumumba of DRC Congo, Milton Obote of Uganda and many others.

Africa also remembers both its current and past world leaders whose looks for Africa illuminate goodness and eludes success, happiness and optimism. A few of them are hereby shortlisted: the 16th United States of America president, his Excellence Abraham Lincoln who proclaimed and pronounced the emancipation of slaves, and stood firm to support slave trade abolishment in Africa and across the globe; the excellence 44th retired United States of America's president, Baraka Obama, an African gene in terms of roots/origin. The African woman who currently holds the symbol of being an ambassador of other African women, her excellence former president of Liberia, Ellen Johnson Sirleaf (the 24th president of her country) who really deserves the **Pride of Africa** for her uncountable efforts to grant African youths with the milestone of possibilities, endurance, devotion and character based on interpretation of others (not gender based or colour based interpretation). Ellen Johnson is an expression of courage, which allows one to wrestle in his or her strength and as she puts forward a smile before the mass of Liberians, especially the youths, she reveals victory and hopes for the future of Africa. As a liberated African woman, she falls no short of experiencing critical moments and unfriendly socio-economic and political conditions (i.e. once jailed and fled to abroad). However, she kept on being bold in order to get into power democratically (from zero to hero), and stands out as a superhero African woman. Today Liberia is one of the leading countries in Africa with numerous improvements in all sectors of life. Now she is retired from politics and its games. She has left a remarkable legacy in the history of Liberia, and her actions have remained in the same position of defining the youth activist. Her actions proved worth when she won the Nobel-Mendel as an award for the numerous achievements she has made in life and later won the Ibrahim-Nobel which more emphasised her best achievements. My Lord, the Almighty grant all leaders of such credit long life and those who are no longer with us - eternal life. For that sensing and logical compatibility, I wish to reward her book in recognition of her activist struggles and for being an African icon.

The Greatness of Tanzania

Tanzania, being one of the African countries has extra things that most of the whole world's people are not aware of. Some of these things are exemplified here below:

1. Tanzania is the only country in the world with Tanzanite minerals.
2. The Olduvai Gorge in Arusha, Tanzania is one of the world leader museums and amazing place in Africa which is historically mentioned to be the first area (in the world) to have had evidence of the origin of man.

3. Tanzania is one of the few countries in the world with lakes containing a variety of natural species.
4. Tanzania is the only country in the world endowed with the second deepest lake with freshwater on earth (Lake Tanganyika) following Lake Baikal, which is found in Russia.

5. Lake chala is the only one in the world with amazing scenery, there is a part of the lake *whereby when you throw a stone, it never sinks into the lake.* It is a lake with no beach. The bottle depth design lake is found in Tanzania - Kilimanjaro region.

Rapid Economic Growth Indicators;

There are enough indicators showing that in a few years to come, Tanzania will be expanding economically from the following reasons:-

(a) Stevirage gorge project (for a strong electrical supply base).
(b) Standard gauge project (this is real perfecting future adequate transport)
(c) Ongoing flyover roads projects in Dar-es-Salaam (this is real showing a rapid economic growth).
(d) Fuel pipeline from Ohima-Uganda to Tanga-Tanzania.

Lake Tanganyika has an area of 32,890 km length, width of 72km and lies in the Great Rift Valley (772mt) with the depth of (1,430m). The lake is inhabited by a large number of Hippopotamuses and Crocodiles. Lake Tanganyika was discovered by David Livingstone and Henry M. Stanley in 1871.

Why was Lake Tanganyika called *Lake Tanganyika?* The name *Tanganyika* is originally rooted from a group/category of fish which were found in the lake. The fish species were called **lates angustifrons** (species of lates perch), which literally mean *Tanganyika lates*. It was then finally put forward by David Livingstone and Henry M. Stanley that the lake would better be called **LAKE TANGANYIKA**.

Illustration 1:1 (indicates the photo of the fish species known as lates angustifrons [Lake Tanganyika]**)**

Tanzania is approximately said to have a population of about 51,046,045 people; whereby about ¾ of the total population are the youths. Tanzania is fond of completing and complementing other people's life fulfilments (non Tanzanians in this case) instead of competing with or against them. For example, Mwl. Julius K. Nyerere once received an amusing request from the Upper Volta (Burkina-Faso) young president, the late Thomas Sankara who said that *"Mwl.... Let me be your son and you..... be my father"*. This quote presents the word of **wisdom** of the late Hon. Thomas Sankara and the message we can derive out of it, is that Sankara conveyed his deepest and heartfelt appreciation of the conduct and personality of the late Mwl. J. K. Nyerere. In other words, when Sankara saw Nyerere in action, he did not only see a leader, he saw a father. To the youths in Tanzania, Africa and across the globe, Sankara's words should be a point of enlightenment/awareness on the fact that it is actions which matter most, not one's physical appearance. In the same vain, Samora Machel who opted to live in Mwl. Nyerere's excellences, the point of view and finally succeeded winning over the colonialists for Mozambique's independence on 25.June 1975. We can also have a look at Tanzania itself; we find a uniqueness that is demonstrated through the presence of 125 ethnic groups/tribes as one of the national assets. The diversity of these ethnic groups is by way of good ideology summoned into one belief of unity, patriotism, trust and commitment towards the national agenda. The tribes speak in one voice as far as the realization of targets and goals for the well-being of national growth. Tanzania is known for the politeness, humble submission and firmness of its people. The values that place Tanzania in the angle of peculiarity are vividly expressed through the national anthem [with beloved song contexts] of *"new Tanzania, new vision, and new youth idea for the new generation; dreaming of a new world of Tanzania" [God bless Tanzania! God bless Africa!]"*. I really submit my interest in and respect to every tribe in Tanzania. I would wish to have all that is needed in order to explore and tell about the historical background of each tribe found in this country. In this part of the text, I will, however, give brief hints on the HAYA historical details. Let it be well known that there are so many tribes which are yet to be known in Tanzania. Because of its smallest in terms of the size of the populace, I pledge you will find it relevant and substantial to know of the Haya and be able to draw inference about the bigger ethnic groups such as Sukuma, Chaga e.t.c. Let's start by observing the following diagram of all the tribes in Tanzania as sketched in the map below:

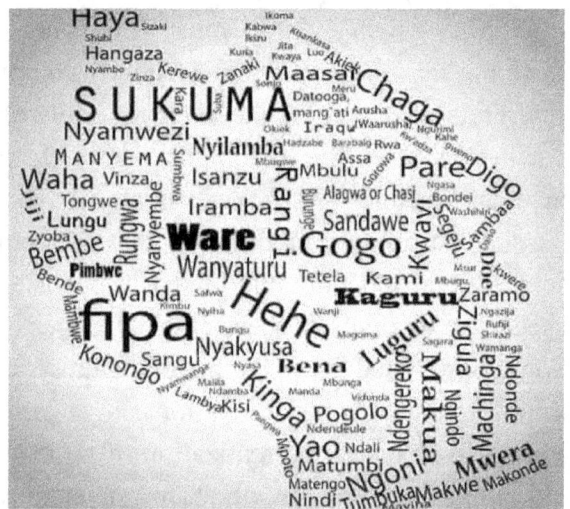

Illustration 1:1

Uniqueness of 125 Tanzanian tribes

1. Alagw(Wasi)
2. Akiek
3. Arusha
4. Aassa
5. Barabaig (Wamang'ati)
6. Bembe
7. Bena

8. Bende
9. Bondei
10. Bungu (au Wawung)
11. Burunge
12. Chagga
13. Datoga
14. Wadhaiso
15. Wadigo16. Doe
17. Fipa
18. Gogo
19. Gorowa (Fiome)
20. Gweno
21. Aha
22. Hadzabe (Hadza & Tindiga)
23. Angaza
24. Haya
25. Hehe
26. Ikizu
27. Ikoma
28. Wairaqwa (Mbulu)
29. Isanzu
30. Jiji
31. Jita
32. Kabwa
33. Kaguru
34. Kahe
35. Kami
36. Kara (Waregi)
37. Kerewe
38. Kimbu
39. Kinga
40. Kisankasa
41. Kisi
42. Konongo
43. Kuria
44. Kutu
45. Kw'adza
46. Kwavi

47. Kwaya
48. Kwere (Nghwele)
49. Kwifa
51. Luguru
52. Luo
53. Maasai
54. Machinga
55. Magoma
56. Makonde
57. Makua (Makhuwa)
58. Makwe (Maraba)
59. Malila
60. Mambwe
61. Manda
62. Matengo
63. Matumbi
64. Maviha
65. Mbugwe
66. Mbunga
67. Mosiro
68. Mpoto
69. Mwanga
70. Mwera
71. Ndali
72. Ndamba
73. Ndendeule
74. Ndengereko
75. Ndonde
77. Ngindo
82. Nindi
83. Nyakyusa
84. Nyambo
85. Nyamwanga
86. Nyamwezi
87. Nyanyembe
88. Nyaturu (Rimi)
89. Nyiha
90. Pangwa
91. Pare (Asu)
92. Pimbwe

93. Pogolo
94. Rangi (Langi)
95. Rufiji
96. Rungi
97. Rungu (Lungu)
98. Rungwa
99. Rwa
100. Safwa
101. Sagara
102. Sandawe
103. Sangu(Tanzania)
104. Segeju
105. Shambaa
106. Shubi
107. Sizaki
108. Suba
109. Sukuma
110. Sumbwa
111. Swahili
112. Temi (Sonjo)
113. Tongwe
114. Tumbuka
115. Vidunda
116. Vinza
117. Wanda
118. Wanji
119. Ware (*the language is like not existing*)
120. Yao
121. Zanaki
122. Zaramo
123. Zigula
124. Zinza
125. Zyoba

Haya's Historical Background.

Haya people originally came from Egypt through Uganda's zone, and then advanced to the place called Kagera "North-West of Tanzania". Their language is not much different from that of the Nyankole people of Uganda. The Bhahaya's main traditional food is **Banana**. The Haya people are proud of being Tanzanians basically because Tanzanian hood cuts out the roots of tribalism. The Haya are said to be like glue as they have offered all the needful circumstances in joining the rest of the tribes in building a sense of togetherness for the betterment of Tanzania.

The Reason Why the Haya Were Stigmatised Nshomile

Nshomile means an educated person (though not all who are currently called nshomile are really educated). The reason for the word 'nshomile' would be traced from the origin of the Bhahaya ethnic group (Egypt). The word 'Egypt' emanates from the ancestor interpretation of unique professionals. This was mainly known as medical *specialization* especially on HEART matters. From this sense, the Haya people, when moved to the Eastern part of Africa, did not abandon the status of being specialists which in their language is perceived as 'nshomile'. Although there are some who practised it and eventually became medical specialists, the word is now used to generally refer to the entire populace of the Bhahaya. So, the word Nshomile is specifically an imitation of the sense of specialization and generally denotes a stereotype of the Bhahaya as a community of the elites.

The Haya community as one of the major tribes in Tanzania comprises of other smallest sub-tribes. These include:

Ziba, Hamba, Nyambo, Nyaiyangilo, Yoza, Endangabo and Kala. Initially, these sub-tribes were not distinctively recognized. They were rather known as groups which constituted a big tribe and their unique identity was not echoed with an emphatic voice. Some years later, every sub-tribe had its own power and independence—each with its own clan chief leader known by the names such as **Mukama** and **Bakama**. The chief clans were fully empowered socially, economically and politically. Nowadays, however, these clans' existence is almost diminishing and the initial past is subject to recurrence in the fact that these tribes are singled out as one group called Haya tribe.

The Haya people's cultural background, apart from being attached to **Bananas**, is also associated with **Senene (grasshoppers).** Senene among the Haya, is a valued thing. In the Bhahaya's worldview, senene is a symbol of respect, hardwork, commitment and love. This sense is an inherited attitude from the community's ancestors although today the attention and value of the senene is fading away as compared to ancient days. Linguistically, the Haya, in their respective groups differ in pronunciations and notations of some sounds. At phonetic level for instance, it is observed that some of the Haya language speakers use sound L in the place of R sound (Lweyemamu instead Rweyemamu). There are also cases associated with ellipsis where some Haya would say Muaya instead Muhaya.

Context and Meaning of Bhahaya Names

Generally, the Haya are known as a community that puts an emphatic worth on their tradition names. The Bhahaya names are largely context based in terms of their meaning.

- The female firstborn is named as Kokubanza, Kokutangilila, and the male first born is named as Lutabanzibwa and/or Kalumuna.
- If the baby is born after a long time in marriage, the names Mushumbusi, Shumbusho and Rwezaula are the probable names for the male child. If the child is female, the most likely names are Kokumalamala and/or Mkaanguki.
- If the father died while the mother was pregnant, the female child born will be named Kansiga, whereas the male child will be called Kashangaki.
- The baby boy born with legs coming first in the course of delivery will be named Ishengoma, while the baby girl of the same trait will be named Nyangoma. The names of the twins

among the Bhahaya are Kakulu and Kato if they are of the same gender; Kakulu and Nyakato if they are of different gender.

- The female child born after twins is named Kyaruzi, and for the male one is named Mkabaluzi.

Viva!!!!! Tanzania, viva…. Africa.

CHAPTER TWO

RESEARCH METHODOLOGIES AND FINDINGS

The Major Paradigm of the Book

The research data and findings pursued in this text were gathered, interpreted and analyzed in the framework indepth exploration and assessment of people's socio-cultural, political and economic landscape. This book covers a diversity and multiplicity of social conditions principally observed from Tanzanian context in particular and the whole of the globe at large. The information composing this text's content was collected through interviews, observation, personal introspection, documentary review and questionnaires. These techniques were employed in realizing such multi-disciplinary knowledge in the areas of fit & fills of job vacancy's requirements, talents and skills from youths, promotion and demotions, persuasion, cash flow and bankruptcy circumstances, entrepreneurship, procrastination, career building from individuals, domicile and how clans associate in empowering the growth of youth's focus. These are believed to be one of the factors which challenge the transformation of

Africa into the paradise of success. However, some clues as expressed in the following views are worth taking note of:

1. As far as winning in an interview in the face of trained interviewers, this book gives you a room to both sort and iron out such challenging instances as anxiety, lack of confidence and irrelevant responses to questions. The book explores the factors affecting job seekers and provides appropriate means and procedures through which such factors can be handled. Concurrently, this book establishes an argument that the concepts such as LOVE, MONEY and NEPOTISM feature greatly in the challenges facing the African youths, which normally pull back youths' focus unless proper management is applied.

2. The findings composing this text also uncover on the growing syndrome/tendency of employees blaming and raising complaints against employers. Yes! there are some complaints with concepts to be looked at but in another way around, there are some problems being caused by ourselves but then become complaints directed towards the employer. This must be first an individual initiative. Sometimes, you find a person who just lacks enough knowledge or information about the concern challenge. When a person is still upset, he/she is

again not in a good position for self-reasoning for resolutions. Eventually, that person becomes the employer's burden. No!! Folks, let us first look at ourselves by evaluating the facts and then turn to employer's side (*what I'm saying here is about checks and balances of the concerns-inverse proportionality*). A cash flow and money circulation at workplace have been endless complaints.

Education and Employment Correspondence

3. **Education**: this concept has been observed with two faces: face one, are those people with formal education. This type of people are regarded as consultants or counsellors in regards to their faculty of study. This type of people are normally dependants over informally educated people. They are not widely knowledgeable of many things apart from specialing some issues of the framework. Then we find informal educated people. This group of people with a world-class education are the persons with enormous knowledge as an attachment to the experiences of life circles. These people are normally ranked as the best performers at workplaces or in the business market because they add value to the products. Their uniqueness is where we found a person holding high position at work with low academic achievements!! This is a

reason of such people leading a group of highly educated individuals.

The photo below is a mine site.

Illustration 2:1

Outsource of HSE & HSSE

All of what is in this book is 95% a real breakthrough experiences that I have physically witnessed vividly. The greatest challenging factor in the mining sector is safety and security works. These two things are like twins; if you are not smart enough you cannot do your work professionally. There are some issues that still need to be worked upon in regards to these two things. As we can see **HSE** (Health Safety & Environment) and **HSSE** (Health, Safety, Security & Environment) these are not two different departments, it is one but incorporated together by SAFETY. Earlier on, the mining sector had a theft crisis before G4S security company lunched effective and innovative security solutions in that industry, this company has really tried to manage and minimize the mining theft crisis though there are some minor challenges still exisiting which have ranked the company as the premium security service provider in some areas. What I have experienced from this particular sector also seems to be an African or world challenge from mining industries towards world millennium goals. It needs a world youth's inputs to regulate environmental circumstances and it is possible….yes it is possible, through skill, talents and knowledge invested in youth.

As the bible says from Proverbs 4:13 "please enrol into education as to be your lifesaver". Together we can do it.

4. **Operations** is a work structure put in a place. This is another angle where work performed is hardly trying to be enough but in some points failed because of:-

    (a) It has been observed that some of the operation managers lack technological skills (meaning computer application) which are very important in putting him or her in a position to well serve the customers.

(b) In another circumstance, a person may keep concetrating on outside activities instead of having some time to sit down and evaluate the importance of those activities with technical reports down. Meaning a person needs to have time for outside operations and time in the office, these two things need to be equally balanced.

(c) A person must stop running throughout believing that it is the best way of pursuing the plans. They must stop sitting in the office throughout and remoting the work electronically. They must stop talking more than listening; this is why human-being has one mouth and two ears. They must stop making decision from hear says. They must investigate and put down the written facts, more especially where there are an incompatible incidences.

(d) Stop being principle centred, if you really want to learn more and make the difference, be generous, stop undivided attention to the people.

(e) Stop talking about work to be done; being a good planner but poor at action talking does not bring results.

CHAPTER THREE

CAREERS

What is a Career?

A career is the combination of two things (internal profiles & External profiles) in Swahili called [*wasifu wa ndani na wasifu wa nje*]. Career is an individuals assertiveness on developing life numeric guidance which influences somebody's path especially on job roles. Remember no college or university teaches career; *career is the only thing, owned by you but your salary at a company work is your job*. Just consider that a career maintains your job security. Career is something like God's gift awarded to a person.

How careers are created?

Career is a certainty of putting into action; plans, goals, visions, missions and values; with an extra ability (talent & skills), whereby you need to be able to collect enough information as it becomes more helpful and effective on addressing problems, making decisions and designing a strategic path to achieve more (that is career creation).

How to Maintain a Career
Careers can be maintained by yourself for creating an environment of gathering as much knowledge as you can from many different sources with attachments of (*humbleness, courteousness, affections, worthy, integrity and perfections*) you need to be well stuffed, by doing so, the workload will be like spiritual auto connection done, as a results your insights will explore towards your goals than thought might be.

Career Strategies or Management
When talking about a career, we mostly apply individual talents, skills and exercise them through self-**career appraisal** and **Career Exploration.** Likewise seen career being the unique thing to a person.

Careers are Made up of:
  (a) **Priority objectives**: this is the best gear after creating a career, then you need to put them into action by following your values, interest, abilities, talents and skills.
  (b) **Gathering information:** a person of values, interests, abilities, talents, skills plus knowledge (education) knows well the down-led procedure in pursuing something that inspires him/her; this is called **insight.**
  (c) **Realistic:** this has been challenging to most people; you may find a person after being

inspired by something, then shortly things die few miles ahead because of something called **PROCRASTINATION**. Or bypassing the titbits, these things real stifle the career path, which allows the devil to enter into the plan and kills all focused targets.

(d) **Options around;** during career management or strengthening, you need to invite as many experiences as you can that you have learnt in the past, which will lastly give you the best layout of endeavour from skills, knowledge e.t.c.. You don't need to select a job or work to do, at the initial stages of building a career if you really want to create an authenticated career.

(e) **Strength and tactics:** if you want to stand upright and maintain job security, you need to set varieties of work strength tactics "this involving spiritual emersion" this is turned as technocratic system from above especially easily done from a God fearing person.

Career; as to be a real career, it needs to be well and deeply processed.

The Career Processing Gears are:
1. **Values;** is the standards of an individual to underline the sense of honour in achieving their targets by clear viewing job security and so forth.

2. **Interests;** this includes talents and skills that were built in you at the time you were born, remember talents and skills are those things which bring something known as INSPIRATIONAL (*you need to aspire as to inspire before you expire*), after realizing the above, then expect marvellous things to happen.

3. **Personalities;** this can also include introvertive and extrovertive, determinations, flexibilities, dully or stubborn. Remember personality depends on how you manage your perceptions.

4. **Abilities;** these may include, verbal resolutions, writing skills, agility, adaptability, physical strengths, application of technological skills.

5. **Lifestyles;** this depends on how you set your life dimensions and hobbies (leisure).

How to Restore a career if it is lost or undiscovered?
There are six things to do, during knestling a career;
1. Review your personal life history.
2. Keep records of references for building your capacity.
3. Review your low and high expenses, expenditures and adventures.
4. Review your satisfaction and dissatisfaction with your current and past roles at work or self-works.
5. Ponder address details of your ideal job.

6. Describes personal life on merits and demerits factors.

How a CareerPromotes a Person.

If you really want to grow high at work, then set a clear path of your career. There are three types of promotional career options. Among these, no friendly promotional grievances or complaints.

1. **Repeating boss' false assumptions;** if your boss made administrative mistakes, do not correct him or her instantly. Take note, some bosses work with opinions of others while others don't. It might be your challenge seeing job standards or KPI not being followed but emotionally, reinstate his arguments and then try to advise. Do not force things, this will give or allow him or her to re-correct. Obviously this is the third eye of promotion.

2. **Examine the facts;** remember when you want to meet your boss, make sure you collect a full package of information or more. This means that you need also to have information that might not be important but is work related. This will give more room for you to explore beyond the target. And obviously this might be potential for anything sensitive that needs a smart person like you. This is perhaps another potential promotion step ladder.

3. **Implications;** this is your comfort zone to shoot overall, just master ways of foreseeing issues and advising in advance. Your assessments and determinations must be high gaged; of course you will be disagreed and be embarrassed sometimes but do not give up. Don't force things to happen, remain firm and always control your temper because soon or later, you will be a king of problem solving and people will queue to you for the sake of counselling and seeking advice.

How Cleanliness becomes a Career Promotional Attachment

This is another area which is very important in maintaining your career. Cleanliness has been a big challenge at workplaces and can be grouped into categories:-

(a) Cleanliness which considers dressing and departments. This has let down many youth in terms of focus after realizing that they are missing something that is work-related. Particularly or casually depressing because of negative comments from people, it causes a person to lose attention.

(b) Mouthing-Smell; this is a challenge whereby youth at work lose marks unknowingly and it might not be easy for somebody to publicly manifest it to the another but it secretly diminishes your performance and perception.

(c) Clean desk policies; you may find a person losing his new position or work simply because of the environment of office table. The table looks like an incinerator or garbage place. It even sometimes goes further to sharing an account on a computer which is pre-informed not to be applied even if the computer is left with an open account unattended to. It might be taken simply as long as bosses say it once but it may really kill your job.

20 Self-Assessment Questionnaire

If you want to grow enthusiastically, please examine yourself with these twenty (20) self-assessment questionnaire:-

1. Do I have financial records/cost effective records?
2. Have I already balanced my books/operational books?
3. Have I been attending even one seminar session per day or month on operational management?
4. Is there any investment made; either mental investment or physical investments?
5. Are there any loans? And is it payable if not, why?
6. Do I really know my correct and right worth?

7. Am I satisfied with my salary/ business income?
8. Is there any control measures put in a place of financial survival?
9. What is my money regulator in daily expenditure?
10. Do I really know my budget priorities?
11. Is it true that I spend higher than what I earn?
12. Is it true that I normally borrow money from my family or friends?
13. Do I buy things out of my listing or a bit higher?
14. Do I re-think on the major purchases?
15. Do I diversify my investments?
16. What are my major purchase methods? Do I have a credit card?
17. On work or finance, do I have a professional adviser or mentor?
18. Have I well prepared the plans or plans have prepared me? (meaning that you will be doing is what you planned or you will be surprised with unplanned outcome).
19. Do I really have my children plan in connection to what am doing?
20. What is my charity shop?

Problems affecting career and has been a promotion killer.

1. A person (an employee) with **excuses**, it has been a normal thing for an employee logging repeated excuses beyond limits. Remember,

sorry *doesn't make a man*, those logs might be based on; for instance,

(a) I am sick (time to time reporting sickness [no month down without one sick report]).

(b) My relative is sick or dead [sorry permission please].

(c) Sorry, I have a family problem.

(d) Exceedingly out of time frame (either from leave or whatever [sorry am late].

2. Failure to maintain effective communication during an emergency.

3. Applying personal problems to workplace like money deficits, marriage issues e.t.c.

4. Lack of business language skills.

5. Jokes oriented. This is a habit where people misinterpret very important things for fun situations. You find a person doing things but they really don't want others to know when astonishingly found. You will hear them say, "oh! I'm joking".

6. Attention to details (exceptional focus and scanning the possibilities).

7. Laziness is sometimes very hard to address, this has been a chronic problem especially at the workplace; this is when a person runs important things by a stagger, which is always difficult identifying the reason. It might be from graudges or gladness of power, position and

dates or otherwise. Whereby work lags behind....... (underground strikes).

CHAPTER FOUR

YOUTHS AND WILLS

Dear youth of Africa; I am herewith honour sharing with you a youth's wealth perspective. First of all, wealth wills are corresponded from the love of parents, granters, sponsors or heritage inherited from those mentioned who normally provide wealth support to the dependants. Also being well dedicated to all holy books whereby people around the world actively respect and obediently responds to them.

Heritage Process

Wealth inheritance has been accounting for lots of laughter within youths and puts a life smile into youth lives; mostly being the best gear of a new life's page of many youths. I just wanted to testify something from this particular area, as I said from my biography, the logic of today, things are quite different from those days; inheritance has become a source of family conflicts in which siblings disintegrate and get detached from each other, relatives are divorcing and trespassing into widowed families e.t.c. Things are ready falling apart today. Let this be your individual governance in decision making. But I am advising you <u>my brethren,</u>

youth of Africa and world at large, let us not concentrate on the our parents' wealth aiming to minimize family problems which are in our day to day lives. This has been a big problem especially in rural areas where a number of activists are not equipped with the heritage material claims. I am a member of wealthy victims, what I did is what I am also trying to advise dear youth around the world.

Material Possession.

Dear youth of Africa let the world know that, my late father at his last day in this world was in possession of **SUZUKI** farm-bike (motorbike), business coffee farm, tanning-bricks for building houses with a concrete foundation. He also had a big carpentry workshop at home. My late father had also go-down facilities at Kemondo-bay and branches at Kisumu-Kenya, Rwanda and Uganda. After his death, things were slowly diminishing and as of today, nothing but scrappers of sites as commemoration. It is actually a long story that I don't want to remember. Reference has it that it was a road accident which caused his instant death.

Wills Confiscation.

Writing this book is to encourage you my dear brother or sister who might be going through family problems resulting from wealth destruction. Please take considerable measures to assess the possibility, if there are soft ways for you perceiving your worth; that is well and good. But if there is some difficult, then God has a reason for you to leave the family wealth because there might be something special and unique ahead of you, so be passionate. Heritage laws and procedures are stated clearly but bypassed and ignored in some way. If you will need to jump into laws and procedures, it will distract and stifle your life focus. Of what May be what God wants you to be in the world, concentrate on your talents and skills? These will give you more features of worthiness than what will take your joy away. Finally, if you engage in such clan conflicts, it may cause everlasting curse within siblings by which even God removes what was planned for you. And if this situation is not well managed, you may end up ripping to see death instead of life; if you are in such category do not generate nagging questions, focus on your second option of life.

The Youths' Greatness.

African youths! Please speak, recite and recycle your inward awards with these great words *"I am great, special, unique and different" so and so...."* This is called God's gift rewards for your strength, May God endlessly bless you.

CHAPTER FIVE

MANAGEMENT AND LEADERSHIP

What is Management?

Management is unlimited application of principles set by administrations, relating to the function of Control, Coordination, communication, Pro-activeness, Reading, determination, Organisation and Planning, as to coordinate the framework strategies of the work features.

What is Leadership?

Leadership: can be defined as a **PTZ** ([Pan-Till-Zoom] this is my idea as I have been a CCTV operator; meaning, you can zoom anything at any time from any angle of the subjected area with leader intents). By the way, remember that leadership is not a maintenance of followers but it is the ability of turning followers into leaders *"leadership is ability of transforming people from followers into leaders"* it is a thing that can be owned by anybody regardless of whether you went to school or not; it is sometimes difficult for a person to identify how it works easily because some people *"do*

*EXPECT of what they don't **INSPECT**"*

Who is a Manager?

A manager is a person holding fundamental principles of work standards, classified with borderless power, enrolled as to apprehend the focused operation targets through Controlling, Coordination, communication, Pro-activeness, Reading, Planning and evaluation.

Who is a Leader?

A leader is a person with wide knowledge, creativity who sets an example through Controlling, Coordination, communication, Pro-activeness, productivity, Reading, determination, Organisation, Planning and evaluating as to spearhead the fits and fills as per operation requirements, while correcting faults as to a refined vision, mission and core-values with innovative spirits aiming to achieve beyond borders.

Just keep in mind that a **Manager** is normally not a leader but a **Leader** is a manager. *You may probably get confused a bit by this sentence but take time, read management books, newsletters think and re-think well, you will find it clear.*

Concepts of Leadership.

Leadership on the other hand is influence. Anything

we might be doing inspires people and influences them; influence means **CONCEPTS** which come from two words put together- **conform** and **transform**.

1. **Conform: -** means anything we engage in, must have the inward oath of the realistic assurance to the people which makes you a person of comfort.

2. **Transform:-** This is an area where an individual striving to change followers into leaders perspective by skills, such kind of people are classified as a humble person and characterised by *"giving...giving....giving....and forgiving"* than getting and forgetting, this is actually God's spirits.

A leader is a person with a **VISION.** Remember that a leader with two visions is a problem because two visions will bring division which will create divorce (**destruction**). Therefore in order to avoid this division, decisions must be done from the heart, not from the head to come up with a **common vision**.

What is administration?
Administration is the hierarchy of grouped order of people with vision, mission, and goal-seeking plans. Administrative components are phrased with indemnities in a strategic manner. Therefore, administration is similar to an engine with gears in the key point of operations.

Difference between Management and leadership.

Management and leadership are terms with long definitions; there are so many things to discuss about these two words but let us go through some of them. Management is made from the administrative platform (executives), a panel which is normally made up of few people who are strong and powerful with a remote control system of work. This enables them to drive a large number of people within the company or organisation. Management is a combination of **administrators** and **manager-activities**, so the manager is a key administrative personnel while the leader is key personnel for operations who often links workforce, managers, administration, C.E.O, Directors and MD's e.t.c. The leader normally meets challenges while manager meets stress. This is because of Administrators being with none principle structures. The administrator is a pinpointed personnel from executives board as to set technical sharpened skills. The position and ranks mentioned need a person of intelligence, smartness, brilliance and with extraordinary thinking capacity as we have definitely seen in earlier definitions of who is a manager and who is a leader. Consistently remember, leadership is a ladder step for managers rendering management goals. The leader is a rank linking operations issues. Dear reader remember that leaders and managers are two different ranks but with same roles. The difference comes with how these two people hold roles and careers. It is very easy to find a leader with managerial responsibilities but it is very rare to find managers with leadership responsibilities, though it happens.

Management is again stated like a strengthened power with inverse proportional (rear/fore) movements that are more featured by managers who are normally called **bosses**.

Dear fellows, from the above briefly explained factors that distinguish managers from leaders, let me figure out something here... In the field sometimes things become difficult when a manager presses down an order and the order meets a person with managerial characteristics. I think you get a point there.

Management, as I said earlier is also tuned to be a group or joint venture of people from the bottom to top ranks. Normally management is shadowed powerful features like I said before. I might not well reach an end of *management* and *leadership* but you can have something of value which may assist you in one way around.

Leadership Abbreviation.

L = Loyalty means be up and down.

E = Energetic means you need to set the pace.

A = Approachable means being open when needed.

D = Decisive means make a decision.

E = Example means to set a good one at all time.

R = Respect means respect everybody the way you like to be respected.

S = Smart means be conscious of your appearance.

H = Helpful means be useful to everybody.

I = Identify means you need a thorough planning.

P = Positive means by knowing where you are going.

The difference between LEADERS and MANAGERS

MANAGER	LEADER
Managers count value; some even reduce the value by disabling those who add value.	A leader focuses on creating value, saying: "I'd like you to handle A while I deal with B." He or she generates value over and above that which the team creates and is as much a value-creator as his or her followers.
Managers have subordinates, create circles of power, and count the number of people outside their reporting hierarchy.	Leaders have followers, create circles of influence. The more they do that, the more likely it is that they are perceived.
Managers have subordinates, managing people, directing the way.	Leaders have followers, managing work, showing the way.
Managers investigate with blaming the scenarios	Leaders investigate people, incident circumstances with a way forward
Managers are maximizing business profitability	Leaders invest in people assets

Illustration 5:1

Management challenges

From any management work field, there are lots of challenges which include: - **Money**, **Love** and **Nepotism**:-

MONEY is always said to be a very sensitive thing at the work place and anywhere else. Though money is clearly known in every corner as a precious thing, in mine sites it is pictured differently. over there, money is like controlling people but not all, but this is may be because mining people are engaged in risky work which is the reason why they are paid awesomely as we shall see from personal government characteristics (emptiness). You may still see people complaining of the minimal payments, there are some HR wage issues for instance but when you have time of viewing this in 3D mode; then you will be astonished by what you might see. You will see the following (one side with sundries requirements absolving about 60% of salary, including extension of polygamies, one side of family requirements absolving 20% and investments taking 20% or less than that. Remember, these scales are just a few among many. For those who fall under these scales are those maximizing illegal activities as to maintain the status of their lifestyles, hence is the reason why theft scales in mine sites are overweight.

LOVE, Love (dates) is another big yardstick used to pull down certain company goals. This has been given different and many meanings at workplaces. It has equally affected both sides, and then a slight professional and technical method will be applied following the intended part which will not be easy for the person of intent to jump over and may easily fall into the trap of lover games; with a difficult express-able means from showrunner. Such environments are like the power of money and positions power whereby with a position one side will be inferior with fear of losing a job. So, this may externally force them to join the love games. On the other side, those who stand tall against this may not last long. They might either face an option of resignation, absenteeism or cadre staging-on with common interest of letting job/work go on. They will have passive resistance. This is much more found on mine sites with a group individual confidentiality. And it is not an easily legal expressible thing; it only falls under moral acts; as it is clearly stated from **MORALS (*JUDICIAL*)**. *There might be no soft path to present the issue or courage to sound it up.* Hence may result in company's potential personnel resigning for a different reason.

NEPOTISM; This has truly remained as a big challenge at workplaces as it has been said from the provision above of (*delegating power or describing moose on the table or promotions*) these are also subjected from nepotism suggestive, these are always underlined as barriers to the certain company's goals even by disguising things, though it often happens. Those are clearly observed from the way of how a particular positioned person saw stipulating the code of ethics and conducts, penal codes and labour relations acts referred to the operational requirements. Which is really being bypassed as a result, the company or organisation spends a lot of money carrying out cases which fall under weakened operational personnel. Let us see this logical sentence which I tried to share with one learned boy by asking, *why are people working in the offices {**senior person**} well paid than those who are physically seen working hard {**lower level**}? The answer was {**because people in the office are few and people in the field are many; so the company might run into loss in case of senior flat-rate payments**}.* Yes it has some logic but it is not the right answer. *The answer I thought was, people in the office are like an engine, it needs to be well serviced so as to drive a large cargo on the truck.* It might be different from that but it is always portrayed to the proletarians and outsiders.

What outsiders are interested to see from a person called a leader?

1. **Passion,** a person pronounced as a leader must be a person of passion so as to deliver compassion to the followers.

2. **Integrity,** this is a nice word and most of the people really want to be entitled to (*a person of integrity!*) but are not all living a life of integrity. Sometimes, there is confusion of two words (integrity & reputation). **INTEGRITY** is who we are when no one else is around and **REPUTATION** is what people think we are.

3. **Curiosity** is the ability to explore and think outside the box; thinking in a positive direction (*think big grow rich*) if you are a leader somewhere and you don't think outside the box, then expect scratches which will actually result to blur-blur results and finally cause distraction of your day and lose focus.

Three main leaders' risks by which a leader real needs to know its applications of pursuing job descriptions.

Undertakers: if you know that you are a committed leader, avoid being around people who undertake other people's business. People who always talk about the negativity, undermining your efforts, a goal-seek questionnaire person, a person who anonymously and maliciously tries to throw stones into your way. If you are around undertakers, you may kill your career and stifle your vision.

Caretakers, These are the kind of people who take care of other people's businesses, this type of people always respect people and often avoid undivided attentions to others; caretakers are the person with sympathy, encouragement and courteousness.

Risk-takers; if you are a leader, just count risks to be part of your package. A leader always sets an example. By setting an example, you are really taking a risk because you don't know what will come out after you take the first step out. If you are a risk taker then you must be daring for big results, you will not escape the following:-

        (a) **Stress,** this will be your work flavours because by taking a risk, you can't avoid stresses.

        (b) **Fatigue,** by being a risk taker expect fatigue because this is an encounter of commitments; if you are committed, then expect being tiring with instant exhaustion. Whereby you will experience a fatigue management situation.

        (c) **Criticism;** if you are a risk taker, expect your closest friends/siblings/wife to criticise what you're doing because you are doing it with a third eye which they don't have. And it might even go far to sending you to your grave which you must be careful of.

(d) ***Rejection,*** don't be surprised to meet people side-lining you from the important things. People whom you didn't think they might let you down from constructive targets eventually aren't seen; even those you didn't expect to talk behind your back astoundingly did.

These are the most things pulling back great ideas.

How a person with managerial characteristics delegates power:-

Delegation of power; most managers are very careful and sensitive about taking care of their position compared to their responsibilities; which means that you may find a person working hard to safeguard their position and forget that *"at work we are paid not because of bills after hard labor, we are paid because of the skills displayed"*. Some managers sometimes ignore helpful, talented and skilled people in the field due to being introverts. It is not true that they don't like those people. They seem to manage well work related issues but fail to utilize them well because of the above guidance limits worrying them. Most managers really think having the best figures in the field ends up using ascendance logics within the system. This being their best way to speed up what they think is the best way of silencing those whom they think are opponents which are really whipping the use of talents and skills at work. Finally ending up seeing what we call productivity diminishing meaning B^+ resources with C^- results. Therefore, the company organisation or NGO's achieving less according to the goals in place and as a result, things are seen falling apart, stagnant, dully-work or a potential personnel staging for a queue of resignation.

Moose on the table: most managers are being escaped by the staffs (employees) after they really know no recognition, motivations from committed, strengthened and integrity personnel and real sees being disguised as another person or ascendency application system. It all finally rises to mistreatment, grievances and endless complaints and finally   passive resistance. Whereby this may not be easy identifying the reason quickly, This may result in people working under close supervision, whereby the manager may come up with a termination solution. Unfortunately, the newly hired staff shortly adopts the same attitudes; people may be well aware of the problems but no one will take courage to speak out. The only good indicator for managers to know is seeing people working under close supervision and there might be artificial baptisms from personnel to manager, although it may not be easily identified. Take an example of when a manager holds a meeting with staffs, people may pretend to support what the manager is putting on the table but realistically, they do not and so the manager may be sure of the plan put in place thinking that it will clearly run but the staff know that things will not move as far as needed.

Promotions: This is another area where the successful fruits are normally considered. Some of the senior personnel (managers) from certain industries play a nice game with no referee involved; sorry about that mysterious sentence that might be misunderstood. I want to clearly show you something logical. The referee in this particular area is **PERFORMANCE APPRAISAL** but some (managers, supervisors) skip that speed regulator by promoting people following their own personal interests while leaving the professionally qualified people behind. As we might all know that **Performance appraisal** is a guideline of:-
Planning, Organising, Reading, Pro-activeness, Projector site evaluation, Coordination, Controlling, Assumed responsibility, how passes on the blames, doesn't entertain worries, Earns trust.
The senior personnel are not appraised of the mentioned but still expecting big from the field, these are also used as the key performance indicators. This might sometimes pictured by people that are positioned lucratively; those can involve indirect relationships and god-father, these are seen given first priorities in the promotion qualifications and used as muscular position

power to silence proletarians who might not want to remain quiet. The only weapon to put anybody free is integrity.

5P's and 5M's of a person called a leader
5-M's of logical sentences from MORAL DRIVES:-
1. What is **Logical** is not **Practical** and.
2. What is **Practical** is not **Right** and.
3. What is **Right** is not always **Ethical** and.
4. What is **Ethical** is not always **Desired** and...
5. What is **desired** is again takes us back to what is not **Logical**.

As mentioned above, please hold the 5P's in genes as to maintain good perceptions on pursuing your plans. We agree that perception is dangerous if it is not well managed it becomes your reality. Remember to maintain your first image on anything you might have engaged in! Below are the 5P's:- (first image symbolic).

> **P = Power**: - Avoid holding power as the best docile
>> gear of life.
> **P = Property**:-Avoid property being the ruling life
>> farms.
> **P = Prestige:** - Avoid being special than others.
> **P = Popularity**:-Avoid being a person who
>> invests in the influence of others;
> this

always makes people gather
together with devilish advocacy.

P = Pomposity: - Don't even wish to hold information without wanting to be prestigious for the sake of publicities.

Leader with self-management:-

Self-management. If you discover who you are, then you don't need to prove anything to anybody about your inward gold coin because the truth will reveal itself soon or later. After identifying this, take private time as to finalise who you are on your own. When you finally see it clear, you will need to stop **COMPETING** with people and instead you will need to **COMPLETE** and **COMPLEMENT** people. And invest much in impartation before departing. I wish to illustrate a bit about this; we labour a lot to better our own daily lives but it is not a good enough reason as to why we are paid or deserve what we earn, no! It is because of skills and talent inputs. Leadership is the ability to transform people through skills. A leader who well knows the word called *logical concepts* (five M's) is well availed with logical/ mental balance. Example:-
I finally recommend myself that "I *am a master of my fate and captain of my thoughts*" by overseeing changing of ranks from **GREAT** to **SIGNIFICANCE** levels. Revealing this, a person must have an extra ideal of supervision "SUPER-VISION".

Dear reader, remember when we were born, talents and skills were built in us by God. So it is upon us to pull them out for the benefit of others.

Four (4) mandate skills of the best leader:-
<u>Communication skills:</u> dear friend, remember that there is power in words. You need to be careful and smart because when you **TELL** you don't just tell but you **SELL** words. These words can kill or heal and therefore as a leader, you need to be more careful. Just know that leaders are the world's great communicators who should always maintain positive communication. For instance, the use of statements like, "well done, good job, keep it up..." You should declare interest to a person of the positive words like, *"you're great....,* *deliberately things are finally done...., you did the* *best...., so on and so forth"*. This is the positive communication which always brings massive results in anything.

<u>Listening skills:</u> most people fail to reach their customer expectations and projected goals. They fail to identify the type of customer and the right way of listening to them. Customers are grouped into five main categories (5) which are:-

    (a) Internal customers.
    (b) External customers.
    (c) Child customers.
    (d) Wife/husband customers.
    (e) Girl/boyfriend customers.

All the above mentioned categories vary from one group to another during communication. You need to be well postured on how you might talk or listen to them and either how the listeners catch the context of your message.

Productivity skills, This is a conjunction of two words **PRODUCT + ACTIVITY** meaning any work we might engage it must produce results. People do forget that ***Business*** means ***Effectiveness***; you may find people who are busy but not effective.

Time-management skills; you will need to have a timetable of all that you want to do. For example,

HEALTH TIME	WORK TIME
FAMILY TIME	FUN TIME

As leaders, we sometimes suffer on how to balance time, and if we can't manage it correctly it may affect our future; example:-

$\dfrac{\text{Work time}}{\text{Family time}}$ = **public successor and private failures.**

Remember, under public successor and private failures do not forget the time of your death, people will end-up writing a nice letter -"*REST IN PEACE*" and you will only leave a fresh memory to your wife/husband, family, children, nation and your friends.

Teamwork skills. **TEAM**-work (Together Everyone Achieves More). This is the best-gifted working gear. It is very rare to find it and this is not even taught in any college or university because teamwork is always built on the base of commitment and goodwill.

One day I met a passer-by whom I viewed as a person with a sharpened mind and I successfully asked him why white people commonly work together as a team. The answer I got was, *"you know why?" he asked again! I answered no! He then said that "white people's brains work thoroughly and in permanent sets"* I again asked why African youth and don't do it too! The answer was, *"90% of Africans mismanage time." We have African time and whites' time. Another thing is general jokes; we much respect jokes. You may find somebody doing something purposely and when, they may confess [am joking].*

Let us see another good example; I came across a note one day in the newspaper, *Look at Indians who are sophisticated and careful, do not wonder, in some years finding them taking over most of the things around the world, let us recite on the street these words saying-* **if you find yourself lost away and you meet an Indian guy and ask for help**, *the instructions will be like this; [turn right.....right!.....then left.......right!....right.....left....right!]* you may end up laughing about the instruction, just take it into reality).

Oh! My beloved Youth of Africa, we have slightly let time out from us, remember "time is money" hence we are obediently allowing money fly away from the opportunities, and sometimes we still complain of money deficits. Let us wake up by joining together with God's advocacy. This will assist us to manage our full potentials.

10 Qualities of a Good Leader

Planning:- A good leader must be able know how to generate new imaginative ideas. They must have ability to resolve circumstances of non-routine nature. They must possess ability to set clear objectives, ability to see a task in its entirety as well as commencement, ability to consider all available information before making decisions and ability to systematically embark from work.

Organizing, This is another key role of good leader; He or she needs to show technical changing circumstances, ability of new inputs with new methods/procedures as to improve work performance, ability to determine activities needed to finalize tasks in an orderly manner, ability to utilize available resources with triumph results and ability to ensure personnel are qualified for the tasks at hand.

Reading: A person with leadership intents must be able to read well, able to apply initiatives, able to delegate power, able to accept authorities and set standards for subordinates.

Pro-activeness: always resumed responsibility, ability to manage time and decisions, avoid being principle centered, trying enough to perfect things and clearly set path following company or organisation goals by grading the standards from KPI (*Key Performance Indicators*).

Projector site evaluation: A leader must spell well on the communication, extending knowledge and experiences to the subordinates, looks over the standard of work, loyalty being a part of life, looks well on judgments, eagerness to undertake assignments and lesson, cooperation being a part of his/her package.

Coordination: a leader knows well how to create teamwork, knows how to control the flow of work while maintaining harmonious, technically switching from one work to another.

Controlling: This is something originally planted to a person, which is a result of commitment and goodwill. It is an ability to give factual information at specific time, ability to take prevention and corrective action, ability to maintain disciplinary standards and uphold them, ability to set cost-effective measures and ability to underline company or personal assets/property.

Assumes responsibility: A good leader is one who tries hard enough to fill gaps by not conditioning his or her services to anybody. This is the point that shows he/she is capable of the procedures, penal code, code of conducts and how they resolve problems.

Do not pass on the blame: a person pronounced as a leader never blames others; remember if you blame someone, you give the power to change. So do not worry be happy.

Do not worry, worrying is the bedrock of vision and interlocking goals.

Earn trust: learn how to earn trust; remember anything you do must be subjected to trust-ships, which will lastly give worthiness.

Note: If you want people to trust you, share information; don't hold information and just care for people. People don't want to know how much you know until they know how much you care. My advice *(if people backbite you take it in a positive way and know that you are ahead of them; that's why they talk behind your back)* remember that what we do for ourselves is gone when we die but what we do for others will remain as a legacy.

Eight (8) Types of Friends

A good leader always knows the best way to spot-check the types of friends; now let us look at some of these types of friends:-

Promotional friend, a good leader must exactly be aware of the varieties of friends and the best way to treat them. A leader who doesn't know how to pin point friends must expect to reap failure. A promotional friend is a person who brings 30% of true stories and 70% of made-up stories or 50/50% stories that might not be work-related issues.

Show off friend: This type of friend only cares about being seen by others; if that is a leader's friend, it makes him/her happy at work and even feels alright.

Retaliation friend: This is a friend who always looks at the angle of the leader's muscle as to easy get compensation to his/her opponent, it may differ in interests or personal issues, "revenging person".

Common interests friend: This is a person who normally minds about what the leader needs which is also affiliated with personal intentions that he/she can share with the leader; for example girl-boy relationship.

Double dealer friend: This type of friend is pretends to be a good friend of yours while maliciously collects gigs from another side. Double-dealer person is clarified with two face attitude in anything he/she might have done. This person always wants to reveal integrity to the mass but their actual reputation is different..

Anonymity friend: This type of friend is classified with good sense and is a person who works with focus, working with ownership spirit, commitment and goodwill but remains anonymous. This person is actually characterized as a God fearing person.

Money oriented friend: this type of friend is resembles a promotional friend. They only differ in perceptions. Money-oriented friends are much interested in money than anything else. They may make up a lot of lies as long as it can produce money for them. This person is also known as back biter, gossiper and mouth sharpener. This is a dangerous friend.

Hippocratic friend: This person is tries hard to make friendship in a courtship way but it is very difficult to control or monitor him or her. This person is classified with two faces but is not easy to identify him/her; you might be in a long-term relationship with him or her without knowing what they actually mean to you as friend.

CHAPTER SIX

STATE GOVERNMENT AND
PERSON/INDIVIDUAL's GOVERNMENT

Dear folks; it has really shown that in the life's circle there are only two things compelled together with different governance system. Those things are **STATE GOVERNMENT** and **PERSONAL GOVERNMENT**. Let us see how it looks like:-

Example of state government sketch map structure.

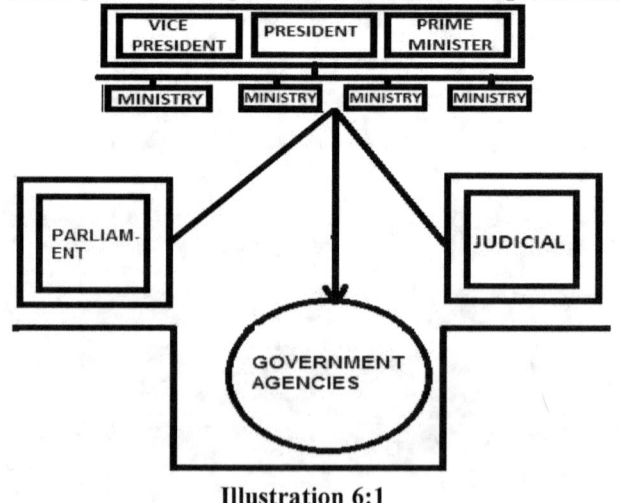

Illustration 6:1

PERSONAL GOVERNMENTS.

Dear readers, you may not much hear this in the best way presented to you now. Well, we'll know the word **government** on the particular state which is being set by the state or nation as sketched above. Briefly on the personal government, I am not good in the state-government expression so I just want to give the difference. I just want you to have a real picture of what a personal government means for you to have a helpful context.

Explanation of personal government sketch map structure.

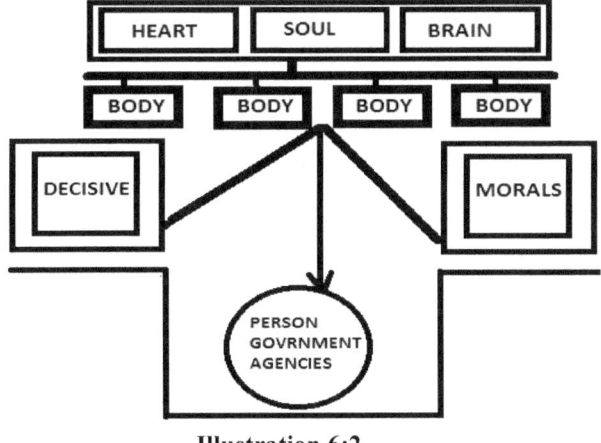

Illustration 6:2

Individual as personal government.

Dear reader, I have tried to collect pieces of information together to bring to your attention for the concept of contexts of the message. If you want to know your inward administration (personal government), you will first need to be availed with the following:-

We'll agree that at the time you were born, talent and skills were built in you. Then am going to show a little bit of personal government as stipulated and how it works.

SOUL-(*PRESIDENT*):- This is a very sensitive unit within a person. This unit is technically owned by God through a person giving full responsibility of management and what to fill in it. SOUL (PRESIDENT) as it has been sensitized with the secretary named **SPIRIT** who never lies and keeps whatever you do whether you are right or wrong. The spirit will keep pressing an alarm on your own of what exactly must be done. This is subjected to a **personal government agency**. Within the spirit, there is a silenced thing called **Emptiness** but with super-powers. This is how emptiness works, it always gives wishful lists, receives it and shortly devalues it and looks to another new thing great. This is a reason why a person is never certified but can only have self-satisfaction by exactly knowing how to manage this meaning of self-control.

MORALS (*JUDICIAL*):- This area is where disputes and long debates are made before. As all we know judicial is independent department and has its committees that works after the sanctions being made by (decisive/parliament) in personal government. Moral acts are held all of through independent departmental, like examples shown below:-

> **Hungry**; feeling to eat something, is morality attitudes.
>
> **Temper**; a level of losing and controlling temper.
>
> **Sympathy**; having much care for other people.
>
> **Empathy**; putting yourself into someone's shoes (act to the problem as if it were yours).
>
> **Trust;** It is a high degree of integrity.
>
> **Grudges; It** is a product of behaving greedily.
>
> **Spirits;** it is innocently; just only waiting for anything as from personal government sanction.
>
> **Love;** is inward acts which work underground and thereafter physically appears and remains Very confidential.

HEART (*VICE PRESIDENT*):- It is a receiver and sender of blood circulation. The heart is where oxygen and carbon-dioxide interchange and it is where we get the word super-vision [*senior supervisor*]. The heart (vice president) is treated as a senior supervisor in the human-nature system.

BRAIN (*PRIME MINISTER*):- It is the engine of inverse proportional movements, high speed in the normal and highways and never dislocates. It is again described as *person government agency*. The brain receives the request from **morals** or **soul**, then quickly knows exactly agents responsible (*Hands, legs, eyes, nose, mouth, private-parts, and waste digestive-part as few mentioned*) no agent mentioned here can do anything without Brain authoritative command.

BODY (*MINISTRY*):- This is a ministry assembly office within a person. What I mentioned earlier from person government agency (*Hands, legs, eyes, nose, mouth, private-parts, waste digestive-part)* these are the tenants/renters into the person's body.

DECISION (*PARLIAMENT*):- This is an area where all moral acts are decisively done, as we all know that the power of state justices or judiciary is to be purified by the parliament which is exactly opposite as done in a personal government. All acts mentioned from this article are from **moral acts**.

PERSON GOVERNMENT AGENCY:- This is a womb with a tit and roles of descriptions; those are **hands**, **legs**, **eyes**, **nose**, **mouth**, **private-parts** and **waste digestive-part**. These are under the remote control of Prime Minister (***BRAIN***). The brain always responds to judicial endeavors (DECISION) which result from moral acts referrals.

Believes and   Beliefs
Refer to ancestor's believes it has also today's impact on youth economic developments. Africans have original believes and beliefs which are real supportive gear on the personal government. Africans are believer from three main things like:-

(a) **Society** –This shows whenever you want to do anything, you will think of how the society will act to you but now days this is potentially diminishing.

(b) **Believes** – this means that every person under the sun has their own believes and beliefs following under formal ancestors training either believing in God or gods therefore the result is how to transfer them to beliefs.

(c) **Personality** – This is the way how the particular person values him/herself. I may talk much on this particular area especially for the youth. Make sure that however skill or knowledge you have is demonstrated to people. This will help you gain more and more achievement with it. The more you deliver to others, the more you become an expert and you will strengthen your skills and knowledge. This is obviously God's endowments to you. At this stage, you will bring people together and build a common team work that identifies your values. This is a testimony of your nation's patriotisms.

Below is the illustration of how a triangular life stands in perfecting the daily life bases:-

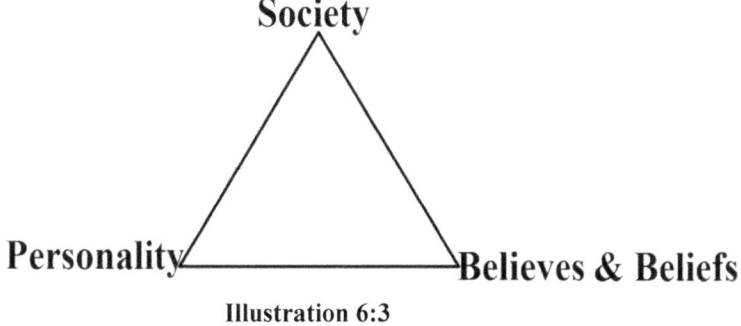

Illustration 6:3

CHAPTER SEVEN

INTERVIEW, QUESTIONNAIRE AND ANSWERS

What is an Interview?

Interviews have been a long and endless journey for many people. Interviews don't have straight answers because it just depends on the person pitching the points towards the bulletin questions and remains on the elevation edge by tackling the relevant questions asked.

Dear job seeker, hiring managers are interested in seeing boldness from the person searching for a particular job. They technically trace who you are through either written or oral questions which will determine who you are and obviously from your outflow, they might know you better. Remember, during the interview you need to be firm, polite and confident. You need to look at the interviewer's faces but do not stare at them. Consider the first interview questionnaire as personality; personality is first fresh bullet from the interview panel. Don't worry about the questions, *"that you might be ask yourself how these questions easily fit for everyone? Since job careers always differ and the same applies to different roles?"* The questions are set in a way of you fitting into them, not the question being fit for you! So by any chance during the interview session, you can win from the design or format of the questions. All questions collected here are those common interview questionnaires although they may differ from the formation but the same logic remains. So do not cram questions or answers please, you only need to know the context. Remember, the job market varies according to the company or organization's nature. There are some circumstances whereby people get employment without an interview or interviewers don't set difficult environments during the interview process. So you may be lucky when you meet such environments. Dear job seeker, this is the way that will put you into the right framework of winning an interview. An environmental circumstance might differ but remains with same concepts. Do not get confused about the questioning styles. There are many approaches of questioning styles but remain with the same logical meaning at your hand.

The only good thing to know when preparing a winning CV is to make sure you are content with the contexts and you remain looking forward for positive results. So, in order for the CV to create a good impression of yourself, below is a vivid example of a winning CV format:-

The format of a winning CV and its credentials

1. Bio-data (personal details); who you are

2. Address. (your contacts, e-mails e.t.c)

3. Personal attributes (internal profiles)

4. Career attributes. (external profiles)

5. Education background (manifestation of knowledge, talents & skills)

6. Experiences (a number of ball kicks you made in your past)

7. Prestige achievements.(promotions or rewards referred to your inputs)

8. Hobbies (inward interests of your fate)

9. Referees. (Pick or point a royal person who will dynamically state facts if contacted)

Illustration 7:1

There are 32 Common Questions from Interview Panels.
This is another area where people or job seekers fail. The proper and technical style to fill job vacancy gaps which will also be right and good stands at going through questions slowly. Remember jobs have been the talk of the world whereby job seekers must have enough knowledge of the best way to cab vacancy gaps

through interview questionnaires. This will be the smoothest entry to the green pasture.

Here are those questionnaires with brief answers, (I *am going to give you the keywords on how to answer them but the answers will still remain with long and deeper expression of you*)

The following are the interview questionnaire and its appropriate answers.

1. TELL ME A LITTLE ABOUT YOURSELF

The technical format to answer this question is "**present-past-future**" formula! Start with your current situation and then explain your past. Pick the *best-experienced work/activities/jobs which express your skills and knowledge*, then finish with future plans of why you are excited to apply for that job.

 Answer: I am a security dispatcher/controller/CCTV operator in British Gas (BG) project but before that, I was the best performing personnel in the mining security industry. After seeing this type of vacancy with the related fieldwork, I find it better to venture out my expatriate works; that is why I am here today.

2. HOW DID YOU HEAR ABOUT THIS POSITION OR VACANCY?

Remember there are three things to consider on answering this question:-

(a) Friend referral; don't feel ashamed of explaining if it was a friend referral gig, " I had a friend from a certain department whom I heard talking about a vacancy in the company/organisation or NGO's e.t.c. This is when I decided to dig for detailed information about your company which has led me to this interview.

(b) A folding spin; you should mention good traits but don't respond out of line. What I mean is that whatever you might have found as information about this company; briefly explain as far as you hope to work for this company or organisation.

(c) Nowhere... heard from no one- just informed; the best way to explain this is, "since it took me a long time without a job, I had to apply to many places and make a follow-up. This is when I met a call of interview for my former advertised job vacancy and it is the reason am here".

3. HOW DO YOU KNOW OR WHAT DO YOU KNOW ABOUT THE COMPANY:

This question is too big so don't look at it as a simple question. You will need to be well prepared. Think well about four things; take a little bit of points from *who you are* [tell me about yourself], then take some points from *why you are the right person for this vacancy*, take a point of *how would you explain the company/organisation* e.t.c. Pick some points on *where you see yourself in five years* to come. All those questions are clearly explained from the four questions;

go through them and it will be too easy to tackle this question.

4. WHY YOU WANT THIS JOB?

Most hiring managers want to hire people who are passionate and job-focused, so the best way of answering this question is like:-

Enthusiasms, during the interview you need to reveal your enthusiasm for the related work of the company.

Rambling, avoid rambling around the answers. Identify the key factors to make roles great, align the experience, skills and knowledge.

Careers; connect to the standard of all your stepping stones as the hiring crew will see you as the only candidate to be hired.

5. WHY SHOULD WE HIRE YOU?

This question is very technical and possibly you might not want to hear it but this is the best question to sell yourself. Remember to consider three things, which are; make sure you figure out well how you will deliver results, how you will exactly cope to the company ethics and cultural background, show that you're the best prospect than the rest of the candidates".

Answer; as from my historical triumph work, it is my key responsibility to my new job position to ensure that the success in fuel consumption is also my best gear of delivering results of the company's goals. Expanding my skills and knowledge in *whatever it might be and adding value into the business market of the company, organisation, NGO, institute or government.* It will depend on the company vision because I am a man/woman who remains active, firm and self-motivated. so I am a problem solver.

6. WHAT ARE YOUR GREATEST OR PROFESSIONAL STRENGTHS?

This is a much-opened question which needs you to share your strengths and requires you to show an eye of entrepreneurial mind-set.

Answer; I have already pointed out my insights of superpower rendering out the required achievements on attending my responsibility. I am self-aware of my focus on a given description of how to utilize my full potentials of careers in the role by moving to the next significance level of production.

7. WHAT IS YOUR WEAKNESS?

The interviewers mostly want to gauge honesty, trust-ship and any red-flag in you. From this question, do not crucify yourself because most people do fail at this area. Mention a positive character that remains as a weak point and show how you deal it;

Answer; well, my weakness is since known I had a knowledge of a refrigeration and air-condition but haven't applied it to the field though am excising on private things. Another example is, it was a pretty scary to speak to an audience but I took courage to speak to small groups which has made me confident to express myself today.

8. WHAT ARE YOUR GREATEST PROFESSIONAL ACHIEVEMENTS?

What the interviewer targets from this question is to know to what extent you are able cast down things that may impress him/her for them to hire you. Show how good you are by collecting all things needed together for perfection while maintaining confidence and confidentiality. Show the way you value the work of the job you are applying for.

Answer; as all my prestige achievements mentioned, (*you can even mention them again*) I will show the difference on the fertile ground to hit the running work frames with awesome work done.

9. TELL US ABOUT THE CHALLENGES YOU HAVE FACED AT WORK AND THE WAY OF CLEARING THEM.

Interviewers want to get a sense of honour from you on how you will respond towards solving conflicts at work. Take in mind that there is no work without conflicts or disputes. Explain the way of handling two conflicting sides professionally hence closing the dispute with a happy ending. This question is still very logical; *make a relevant story*, quickly pass through most challenging events you solved by which of your insight offerings made it possible to get a positive ending. In that story, you will consider three things (*1. Right story, 2. Make a clear statement, 3. Figure out the good ending -conclusion*)

10. WHERE DO YOU SEE YOURSELF IN FIVE YEARS TO COME?

Be realistic of where this job or position might you. Interviewers are concise to see the three things: - a) realistic of your expectation (b) your ambition (c) the way you align goals and growth through your position.

Answer; I am very proud of the position because I see five years of high growth in this particular job and becoming an expert of my company. I see myself taking on more managerial responsibilities and even holding or leading a major company project. I will also be lucky to work with cooperative managers whom I might be free with and fairly grow myself in managerial careers.

11. WHAT IS YOUR DREAM IN THIS JOB?

This is not a very different question from any other you have answered. A better way is to talk about your dream and the key bet is maintaining a positive ambition for the job and as that alone will bring you closer to your dream. The way of answering this dream job question is;-

Answer; skills indents, my dream is to put on the table my best mentioned driven work, which will keep me in the green zone of learning more and being the best that I can be. I am also interested in this job since I know it has got a combination of my fates. My dream also is seeing my values being revealed through what I definitely believe are right skill expressions.

12. WHAT OTHER COMPANY HAS INTERVIEWED YOU?

Interviewers have a reason why they do ask this question. The main reason is either to know how many companies you are connected to in the particular job industry or your context for the industry. The best approach is to tell them the truth of how you have explored other companies in the industry. If possible, mention them. This is like an integral question so you need to be much carefully.

Answers: it was my hope that a call of interview might be coming but I can really tell you; basically what I know for this position is a very and exactly challenges I was looking for a suitable company where my role can fit. Yes, I have been interviewed but it all comes down to delivering an excellent customer experience. I keep an open mind on the best way to achieve goals.

13. WHY ARE YOU LEAVING YOUR CURRENT JOB?

Don't get confused with this question, this is a challenging question; remember to remain positive and exemplary. "I really want and love to be part of the development and very eager to have an opportunity here.

Answer; I took my current job vacancy outright since I am vending for all full potentials and being a goals achievement step ladder. A new manager who was brought introduced a system whereby the straight strategies faded and careers were potentially lost. That is when I started looking around and eventually saw this job vacancy with a career's promotion through vision mission and values.

14. WHY WERE YOU FIRED?

Be carefully while answering a question like this, don't cringe, panic or be afraid but admittedly be honest, remember today's world is small. The sense in this question is logical tones, the pitch of approach and upright statements.

Answer; I am going to give you a skeleton of this question, because this question refers to the causes of you losing your job. Then consider the following. (a) prepare well enough before you sit for an interview of positive answers to the questions (b) use brief and clear explanations of what happened (c) twist yourself quickly (*meaning what you learned and come to the topic on the table*) (d) never bad mouth your former bosses or company (e) remember to mix something funny or interesting.

15. WHAT ARE YOU LOOKING FOR IN THIS NEW JOB POSITION?

This question is not much different from those many asked earlier but be specific and accurate. Do not regard it as a trap, be firm and diplomatic.

Answer; Am going to set dynamically the mentioned skills (*you can mention it again*) where I will courteously exercise them too and again putting in place self-motivations in me in a wide range. I know that in my long-term goals, I need to take ideally control of managerial responsibility in future being at the company. I can see high growth of my particular skills and being the part and parcel of the company's success.

16. WHAT TYPE OF WORKING ENVIRONMENT DOYOU PREFER TO WORK WITH?

Remember this is a question which you must be well aware of the company or organisation you're applying to; environmental/historical background, culture and even ethics before you get to the interview panel.

Answer; I have passed through the company tweets before attending this interview. It is a real favourable working environment as all revealed. I think of adding my skills into the frame. I look for fair processing environments that can bring out the best of me.

17. WHAT IS YOUR MANAGEMENT STYLE?

Dear friend, it is well referred from management provisions above. But let us put lubricants into the engine. Remember a good manager is one who is flexible in twisting at any position; that means you are a manager by rank but you are actually a leader. Spell out the leaders characters.

Answer; I will be styling by giving clear directions while leading by setting examples with pretty handoff, but ready to jump in at any time to offer the guidance, expertise work and help needed. I really look upon what makes me unique and different as to give a clear image of my company against other company service providers.

18. WHAT TIME DID YOU EXPERIENCE LEADERSHIP?

Dear reader, this question is wise, so open and also well explained earlier. Go through leadership as to give a wide range as to explore more and more. Let us see a bit of the question in short.

Answer; are the right answers from question 8, question 10 or question 14. Whatever you will choose one from those mentioned questions answers are all correct.

19. WHAT TIME DO YOU DISAGREE WITH A DECISION THAT WAS MADE AT WORK?

In this question expect nagging statements from another side (interviewers), goal-seeking questions; the only thing to consider is to remain brainstormed, do the best to show that you are the best job candidate. Keep mentioning your prestigious achievements. Pick another story of best achievements. On setting answers by referring to what you explained before, align (*setting a right and good story, first approach of the statement, and conclude strongly by inserting hilarious intents*).

20. WHAT AND HOW WOULD YOUR BOSS OR CADRE AND CO-WORKERS RECOMMEND YOU, IF WE MAY CONTACT THEM?

Do not feel so low; you might think quickly on what

bad things you did a previous job. What is needed in this question is a way of submitting the interests and declare your fortifies. Your brain needs to quickly stand firm for the recent best achievements.

Answer; I really believe they will speak out my recent performance reviewed, (*you may sometimes exactly know how your boss and subordinates normally describe you and then you can also quickly sort for-stance two or three traits and align well to the answer*)

21. WHY WAS THERE A GAP IN YOUR EMPLOYMENT?

This question might be established from your biography presented if at all there was a time period mentioned with unemployment. If you have no gap of unemployment, then the answer is short. But if yes, remember don't blab here and there trying hard to explain why you left a job; the answer might be framed as:-

Answers; I strongly and actively display my uniqueness in my job etiquettes. I remember when the company shot up goals from my inputs of ……. This left an open door for job vacancy wining.

22. CAN YOU EXPLAIN WHY YOU CHANGED JOB CAREER PATH?

Remember this question is so logical, take a harmony pause with deep breath and state with a pitching approach. Take an example out of various skills that you have.

Answers; since acquiring knowledge of (*mention them*)

following skills and talents, this resulted into shaping roles and careers of my present achievements and then I realized the knowledge is banked with less dividend only used as an attachment.

23. HOW DO YOU DEAL WITH PRESSURE OR STRESSFUL SITUATIONS?

This question trying to gauge whether you are the type of person who knows the right things but has no courage. And to see how you are capable of whipping the barriers on accomplishing goals. The **answer** will depend on your working history. So try to configure well the breakthrough conflicts and riots with sweet sided endings. When you will be configuring this question's answer, remember three things; (right, clear and good statements plus smart ending -*conclusion*).

24. HOW WOULD YOU LOOK LIKE AT FIRST 90 DAYS IN YOUR NEW ROLE?

This question is a goal-seeking question and interrogative ideally. So stand firm and have a comfortable approach. Keep reciting and recycle on your achievements.

Answer; for being on a front line and actively responding to the onset goals, I will be also a fresh bullet upon company laid down targets whilst upholding the company standards.

25. HOW MUCH DO YOU SELL YOUR EXPERTISE?

Do not go out of line from this question, it might be

situated in anyhow but the logic is the "salary". You better first find out and search for the company's payment profile, rank specifications and salary scales. Be flexible in case of any negotiations and be conceding of the first offer.

Answer; keep phrasing the best-achieved scenarios whilst mentioning amount as found in your research, either by a bit less or the exact mentioned figure.

26. WHAT DO YOU WANT TO DO OUTSIDE WORK?

Remember this is your CV's hobbies referral question; be careful to stick to the hobbies which build your capacities (capacity building); try hard to sound more professional for instance religious (*behavioral guidelines*) reading books e.t.c.

Answer: Networking; I am interested in making friendship with great people like company C.E.O's and executives. That is my hobby out of work.

27. IF YOU WERE AN ANIMAL WHICH ONE YOU WOULD BE INTERESTED TO BE?

This question is a personality test question. What the hiring managers want is to pick thinking feet footages from you. Remember there are no wrong answers to this question. But the best **answer** of this; you need to be technical grounded, just term it as a bonus question, just smile in a way…, buy time as it might allow. As I said, no recommended answer then just pick the enthusiastic answer which may bring automatic funny being. Then end a sentence that looks like a question to the interviewers. This wholehearted concept will lend your insights which will inspire the interviewers.

Animals express some human traits in real life. That is why powerful people identify themselves with lions while wise people take on the hare and visionaries pick the eagle.

28. TELL US ABOUT YOUR TENNIS BALLS AND RESOLUTIONS!

This is a very bad question which no one wants to meet at all but it happens in interview panel. This is called a *"brainteaser question"*. This question drives straight into the heart painfully; it is not about life's hardness or the hard times you have met in your life circle. It is about what takes down all of your moral units. This is like losing the traits you had. For example loss of beloved mom/dad or something similar to that. The format of answering this question is; first control your moral drives and then follow an assumption trait.

29. ARE YOU MARRIED OR ARE YOU PLANNING TO HAVE CHILDREN?

Remember personal life is not related to the interview etiquettes but it doesn't mean irrelevant questions won't come; questions about marriage, children, religion, and concubines. They are not in any way connected to the job you cited for. What you will need to do is look for the best way to dodge them.

Answer; For example, am always actively pointing my focus of job career and roles and not giving room for family life issues to be wrapped into my job descriptions?

30. DO YOU EVER LIE?

Do not look at this small and short question slightly, in a real sense it is too big. This might be answered from most of the other questions that you tackled earlier. Most people fail to configure this type of question well. They may start nagging the interviewers which might be a reason for being thrown out from job offerings. The only thing you need to remember is, no one under the sun hasn't gone through lies. So just configure your answer well from past experiences either childhood or later years.

Answer; I remember when a boy/girl approached me for purposes of starting an intimate relationship; I told them that I am HIV positive. They easily went away. I lied because it could distract my contractive plans.

31. WHAT WILL YOU DO TO BETTER OUR PERFECTIONS?

This question might be figured in many styles but the concepts are for interviewers trying to see something special which they could interest them. Any company/organisation is so eager to see changes day-to-day from good to great. Obviously, this question might be an ending of the interview; so prepare yourself to embark from the interview panel. Of Course, there might be one or two other questions.

Answer; For example, as having been part of the company's achievements, I have learned lots of new ideas which always put a smile whenever I am given an opportunity to deliver results.

32. DO YOU HAVE ANY QUESTION?

Dear job seeker, this is actually not an interview question; it is for you being asked to conclude or close the interview page. This is your fertile ground to plant your best seeds. There are many great bundles of best questions; remember that there are nine cases that you can pick a question for asking the interviewer. These areas include;

The job itself, training, performance, interview, company, team, culture and next step (*next step is an area for you to ask a question from it*). Below are example questions from each group mentioned above:-

Types of Questions for you to ask the Interview Panel.

1. If I launched the triumph skills and knowledge, wouldn't three months be enough to see the great changes?
2. I am eager to learn every day; will you please offer some training so that I can continuously sharpen my skills?
3. Can I know the first important thing which you could have needed to be the first prioritized in my first 30days?
4. May I know what makes you great what has made the company become big to date?
5. Where do you see the company within a year after vending out my certain skills?
6. May I know to whom will I be reporting to and their greatest challenges?
7. May I know the company slogans and cultural factors?

8. As from my biography, are there any fills and fits of the roles?

CHAPTER EIGHT

EMPLOYMENT

About Employment.

Dear reader, employment remains as a world challenge as we said earlier about the job market. Every country around the world is particularly working hard on the word EMPLOYMENT aiming to equally share the national cake. Many countries still have a number of academia persons who are jobless but still fighting hard to meet job vacancy markets. Some of them are missing the vacancies due to failing to figure out the job credentials needed. By looking forward into youth's success from all angles of the recent new generation with new visions, new great ideas believe that *young people's brains are like mines that have never been mined*. By helping each other we can see some tailored materials of how we can gather together African youth setting one step ahead every day.

What is Employment?

It is the relationship between two sides; the employer and another side and the employee, usually based on contracts whereby one part sets principles of time profitability from one side and other part spends time for earning a salary from another side.

What is the Best way to Get Employment?

Most of the job seekers usually suffer looking for the best way to kick-up the employers' interviews target. Job seekers must first know the best way of digging up gold-points from what the employer wants before getting into the interview crew or cabinets. Just remember the 32 common interview questions.

How is employment beneficial to an employee?

A job seeker after successfully winning an interview will then be called an employee, plus or minus 80% of the employees make a U-turn of vision and mission towards their goals. This might be because they first think of refreshing out stress and hurtled breakthrough in their life circle before getting the job. They forget that once you get a job, instant income expansion starts which is shortly seen at the first being big and suddenly becomes little. Some employees think the project or job will last for ever. They even sometimes see as if the company will be there for ever and so they relax. The company might be everlasting but not your job. You may find a person at work losing their focus from three groups of employees with financial structure from salary earning statistics.

Three employee's financial management groups.

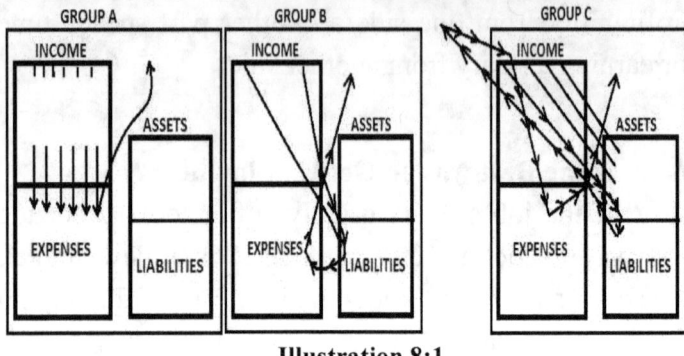

Illustration 8:1

Income: a monetary system whereby a person earns after doing enough labored.

Expenses: is like a vent which slowly or quickly absolves a labor significance gains.

Assets: is anything you invest in for the reason of profit gain later.

Liability: it looks like an asset but depends on how you display money onto; in short it is anything that takes money out, like fashion phones or family vehicle and luxurious.

Let us see these groups **A, B, C** and how they respond to the (**income, expenses, assets and liability**) and am going to deeply explain this here below:-

GROUP A: this type of employee group's salary meets or finds responsibility instead responsibility finding the salary. Therefore, this group's salary is deliberately consumed by expenses. When we talk about expenses here, we mean life's basic needs which are important for any person. But it needs an intellectual head or branstormer. This group never touches **assets** or **liabilities;** this group can be called **low-class** people. This type of people never think out of the box. They are in the economic crisis ever and ever.

GROUP B:-This type of employee group is also called the **Middle class.** This group's salary directly goes to the liabilities; you might be a bit confused about this. It is simple to know it. If he or she gets promoted or any other green pasture findings, what will first come into their mind is fetching a better house (profile venue), private means of transport and other liabilities that don't bring in money. A person needs to look and relook well, think and re-think. If you take a loan and buy a car for a reason of rescuing time, it is good depending on how you invested on time factors but most of the people talk about time but they do not well invest in it. Remember, a vehicle will need maintenance services, fuel and emergencies like accidents which will also depend on the salary that remained after the car loan deductions; house rent might be based on yearly reimbursement but loan goes more than a year. Finally, these two things loop up and cause a stress of a pay day-cheque. Stress will also be doubled after a list of school fees, wife sundries, siblings e.t.c. Demands deliberately depend on that little money remaining. About 80% of this class of people, expenses go beyond income, and as a result, you may find a person full of stress. Though from our view, we see them differently, we see them as blessed ones.

GROUP C: - This group is sometimes called **high class**. This type of people put a plan down before they get money, they exactly know about their plans (if you fail to plan, then you plan to fail) all these two are plans. It is somehow difficult for this type of people to undergo bankruptcy unless of uncertainties. They know of income segments, expenses, assets, and miscellaneous words:-

Income:- high-class people; when receiving money (salary), dividends or whatever it might be, they first think of an asset; meaning they take challenges as an opportunity by looking through vulnerabilities of which important thing to be give them first priority.

Assets: They diligently know how to induce whatever all passes in their hands with an eye of income source; high-class people slowly devolve on the economic growth, they normally don't depend on one source of income.

Liability: provisionally explained above, these are goods things but not productive as we clearly saw from group C. This type of people is a luxurious oriented group but high-class people have a good number of incomes sources and they clearly set one or two sources for liabilities. Finally, liabilities are what generates expenses, this means they take money from you.

Expenses: as explained well above, high-class people

know how to figure out expenses, they really <u>peruse</u> life expenditures with its income break-line.

Miscellaneous: Normally group A and B never know this particular word **miscellaneous** and how it works. Group A and B are always pondering and stressed on how money slides from their hands. They normally comment that money is a devil "*I don't know how money gets lost, possibly bandits steal money unknowingly*". There might be more Miscellaneous explanatory but take into consideration that high-class people know how to value small money but other groups think of that small money as if it cannot do big things. Hence class C group clearly sets an income for an emergency or pocket money or any other good word you may rename it meaning **Miscellaneous**.

How Lazy People Survive at Work.

There are some useful techniques employed by people at work. Outwardly, such acts look good, but in a real sense, they are bad. The techniques include the following:

1. People might be seen busy in the office nested to the computer but actually they might be charting; they only want other people to believe that they are too busy.
2. Look at a person attending a meeting with a huge pile of documents/diaries; if you have time to check what is written in, you will find that it

is worse or less interesting than attending the meeting plain handed (with no document for keeping a reference at all).

3. Others would say, "Oh! I'm busy than ever......" and they may even try to mention the type of work and the time framed for such a work.

4. Leaving the office in late hours and passing via the boss's door/window; this is a way of raising an alarm of hard work.

5. Keeping a number of files and documents on the table; this is to present a stressful administrative work.

6. Converts; goodwill into sacrifice, confidential into secrets, civil issues as work attachments and prioritize as important issues; a lazy person tries hard to give gifts, those may include their own property or offering more time for even unnecessary things.

7. Do not spot problem by thinking you might be criticizing your boss; you might be the first-person to cause problem (*an assumption is a right thing people to know*).

8. During an event (*incident or celebration*), a lazy person speaks more than the proposed ones and also wants his/her comments to be prioritised.

9. Relaxations and luxuries are things given priority on the place where no one else is around

and even sometimes exposing the interest on the massive centre.

10. Do not learn for the reason that people may know that she/he is incapable, so think of risking her/his job.

CHAPTER NINE

THE REASONS WHY BUSINESS FAILS TO GROW

The youth normally have many good plans in the business field but a minimal number pursue these plans well especially when you evaluate the groups of business launchers in period of one year. The following are shortlisted as some factors affecting and jeopardizing youth business plans:-

i. Trust.

This is an attitude that builds itself within a person and it needs more time to be proven by you before outsiders. It is done by telling your soul in every act you engage in. How do you reveal trust? This always lays on the moral act which will finally give you an answer of whether you are trustful or not.

ii. Trustworthy.

This kind of factor hinders many business plans. If somebody trusts you and goes beyond; for example if you find yourself in need of transport to somewhere and your best friend gives you such support with agreement of one hour, if you bring it back in two hours, It might not have effect at that time but it might minimize your worth.

iii. Integrity.

This also a moral driven trait but in different paths e,g this is who you are when no one else is around. Most people normally confuse *trust, trustworthy, reputation and integrity.*

iv. Inspiration.

Sometimes we fail to analyse realistically inspired things and fail to outline them well after being inspired over its branches, just think of *"aspire* as *to inspire* before *you expire"* instead of being inspired from successful people, we do imitate the success. This will be a short term business success.

v. Commitments.

This is a main key point for youth business failure; how to sacrifice oneself, lacking consistent habits and passionate attitudes on the business market. The way you perfect things, it might not be 100% results but it will be on the good stage.

vi. Customer Care.

This is another reason why businesses fail to apprehend their success. Whereby failure to pitch the right speeches to the customer especially to the difficult customers. The language used during running the business is crucial for business growth.

vii. Time Management.

This is the main key of accountabilities to the businessmen/women e.g at what time do you open and close your office/shop. For example, if you are at a location with enough customer base then it is an opportunity for you to get the customers that flow back lately from work and those who leave early in the morning for work, if you can't look very careful at these type of people then you might be left a gold-room door open (business failures).

viii. Time Frame.

What time do you estimate to start gaining profits from your business? This is another challenge of the business launchers. Most of them think of profits after the first three-four days of business, no!no! You need to figure out a good foundation which can start bringing profits from at least one year minimum to four years maximum.

ix. Perceptions.

Remember to maintain your right image within the society/customers e:g dressing and departments, how you dress and compared with your image/personality; bad-mouthing people, bad smelling, deodorant-less, confidence, docility e.t.c; if you will not manage them clearly, then you will be your own business killer.

x. Reputation.

This is like a moral drive belief. It is the tendency of a person creating a false attitude which he/she feels good about but in reality is bad, their original colour is hidden. Avoid mimicking a person but learn from a person.

xi. Financial Records.

You need to be more disciplined in your financial system like making sure that not even a coin passes through your hand without written records of either softcopy or hardcopy; this will help you create a concrete financial system by which this being a very layer of financial freedom. Finally ending the challenge of shorter business existence plans. Below is the example of many sampling financial records.

xii. Life skills.

This means if we really talk about business, we mean effectiveness to collect all correct information related to the particular business on the firm. Most youth do get inspired at the finest stage of business and forget that those fine results come from enough torturing chamber. The most things to consider once you think about starting a business is acquiring the relevant skills and knowledge. And please try your best to use all the knowledge and skills including informal and formal trainings as your business success attachments. We believe all people under the sun have life skills; please apply them on your selected business.

xiii. Respect.

Among the many youth who start their businesses seriously and eventually get well, some change their attitudes after having something in their pockets and they start to undermine other people. This is always killing the business.

xiv. Steps of Marketing and Marketing Plan.

This is another place which is not really handled with care; it is the area which potentially kills the business. The following must be the first key point.

1. The styles used when you move out from the office. "*Shop, company e.tc.*" for example, you may move out intending to do marketing, but rethink if it is well planned financially. Example, apart from planned things like maybe postures, jingle or broadcasting talk, is there extra expense spent? Did you plan over the transport, lunch, drinks or tips?

2. Is there any planned targeted market or it is about moving all around intending to target anyone who comes your way? Don't do that! Is there a written document describing your business?

3. Does your business refer and consider values additional things.
4. Do you have a proposal for current and future marketing plan?
5. Is your business addressed? Do you have business cards, brochures, posters, blogs and websites and to what extent do you interact with the media?

xv. Public relation (PR).

If you don't manage good public relationships with your society then this is another business killer method. The way you integrate with your society on different social activities is the building coverage of your business growth.

xvi. Legal Aspects.

Whenever you think of the business, first think of the authorities towards your particular business permits; it has been a challenge of the business launchers having little information/knowledge of the business concerns which ended closing the business because seeing dully response with you and authority; and referring your business in lawful system managements.

xvii. Believes and beliefs.

This is another issue with a big contribution on the business platforms; this standard of believing in someone as your extra mentor and again attaching beliefs of your soul. Where is it surrendered to? God or witch doctors? Do you know yourself? I advise you to surrender your business to God.

xviii. Values.

This is a tendency of an entrepreneur valuing more money instead of valuing the plan. When you value the plan and you properly put it down, then money comes automatically. Don't think this is to be done when you are well organised financially or materially, no! This is the first stage when you think about business. When you put this plan down, that is when you will astoundingly find some money on your pocket forgotten. This is because you value the plan than money. Some people may comment that you have a lot of money to the extent of forgetting them but it is not true! Money should be your second plan on the economic fields.

xix. Personality.

Your outside view has much contribution on your business market. You need to maintain a serious and smart work ethic. But remember that you don't need to be serious all the time; you will need some time to relax, you need to balance those two things.

xx. Happiness.

In business, happiness is a very important staff to consider. It may happen to be triggered from home, friend, some customer, husband, wife, girl/boyfriend; its temper falls on the business side. This needs high skills of business influence which will dissolve them and finally business remains on the some speed of success.

xxi. Options.

Most business launchers (youth) fail because of being selective instead of managing consistence optimistic perceptions on the right and correct option.

xxii. Status.

We sometimes fail to meet and exceed expectations because we are in the business as a coverage of our life status. For example, your value is seeing people adoring you, so you will be doing business much more covering other people's eyes that look at you. (You are doing business maintaining status).

xxiii. People Selection (vetting).

Most business launchers normally go straight with their first choices of their thoughts instead of having a second time to evaluate them again and again. Thereafter many of them give relatives priority in their businesses; either by planning of minimizing costs or too much care for the relatives. Think about this scenario. If you have two employees; one is your relative and another person who is not related to you; if you find them committing the same mistake, how will it be treated? If you treat the situation rightly, family conflicts might arise because of treating your relative like a normal employee. Finally your business will be in trouble. The experience shows that other person what makes him or her be there and they know one mistake the following is firing action, so they normally not joke around. You need good and enough venting. You can really trust and believe in your people but remember the dream is with only one person....you!!!! (*You can't inspect of what you can't inspect*).

xxiv. Capital.

Capital is a thing that cannot erupt like mushrooms following a person who is highly in need of money. People do complain about capital; capital is available but the way of getting it is the only challenge to most complainers. Challenges are like as follows:-

(a) *Discipline;* remember if your discipline is not well described by your society or even your family, then no one will trust you. Then you're losing an opportunity of either investing in you materially, financially and mentally. You cannot be granted such capital.

(b) *Attitudes;* remember what gives you values is your attitude. My dear reader, when a person is born, there is something special called the **SOUL** in you which enables you to be described before anybody describes you (the soul can communicate from person to a person before they physically communicate) For example, you can comment about a person if they are a drug user, thief, prostitute, good one e.t.c. who told you about them? It is your soul. Manage your attitude and people will assist you in following your dreamlike.

(c) *Friendship;* be keen and smart in selecting friends as we saw the types of friends earlier. When you select the good group of friends, then those are the ones who will take you ahead of your requirements e.g you may be in need of money for rent and somebody offers you a free business room for you to use. Before you get money for starting an ice-cream business, someone may give you their fridge to use. Please be keen on this area of the mentioned types of friends.

(d) *Talent and skills:* these are freely given by God. This is enough capital although most people ignore them and start shaping other careers.

xxv. Budget.

Most of us are not well budgeted on our financial status; money goes and we ponder and wonder how money slides from our hands. If you real mean effective business you will need to regard a budget as your upcoming habits for home expenditures and in business; everywhere, money comes as an equivalent proportional to the plans *"when you talk budget you mean plans and pursuing plans you breakthrough the budget"*.

xxvi. Security.

Most people not consider security very much in a particular business. To what extent do you keenly survey your selected business area about thieves, bandits, robbers and snickers e.t.c.

When you think about the negatives, you will never join the business game. If you find a good place for business with people, then it is your area to prosper by technically taking control measures than to be the best among the failures.

xxvii. EFD Machine.

EFD (Electronic Fiscal Device) is a machine in the ground for some years back and today it has become the country's economic backbone (for tax collection) featuring to support the mentioned country economic growth indicators. If a businessman/woman would well be knowledgeable about that machine, it will double the expected economic rapid growth impact.

The EFD machine as a point of view is not liked by people who are not well conversant with this machine especially about the government system of buying & selling. But in real sense this machine is the best on both sides. The following are the major factors that make the machine unavoidable. Business mechanism nowadays is very difficult for somebody dreaming big in the business industry with a long-term plans, then you must think first of EFD machines. The following are the problems of youth's business planner.

(a) *When Authority says EFD machine is eligible for fourteen million (14,000,000) and above, this as mostly translated negatively*; meaning that people do count this amount as initial

capital that you need to have, that is when you
can process the machine. In the real sense, TRA
calculates your daily sales on a yearly basis with
the sum of such amount. E.g. a person with
daily sales of **50,000 x 6days x 4weeks x
12months equal to 14,400,000m.** This is
beyond the imagination of how the machine is
unaffordable. After having this awareness, we
can think and rethink on the business expansion
methodologies.

(b) When a person launching a business aims to
perform higher, EFD machine must be
prioritised. This will be a helpful plan for
meeting the target. Remember where we are
now- no EFD no business.

The word TRA (Tanzania Revenue Authority) might
differ depending on the country itself.

xxviii. Giving.

This is another area business launchers forget.
When you have a tendency of giving, it
becomes a gateway of shooting above. This is a
Godly gift in your business. This is a very
challenging area you need to be much careful
with. Christians know about tithe (one-tenth). It
is an example; it goes further ahead by helping
none life supported. Do not think that giving to
your relatives is also considered as tithe, no! Be
a helper to your society; remember to avoid

being a person with characteristics of getting...*getting...getting and forgetting!!!* But just be a person of *giving...giving...giving... and forgive!!!* I don't mean that you should not save a profit of your business, no! no!. Some people give beyond comparison; it will kill your business and others never give which will take away the blessings or the business will never grow.

xxix. Training.

Try your level best to attend trainings e.g seminars, business groups, joining entrepreneurship groups like, Facebook, Inspirational talks session seminar and WhatsApp individual groups e.t.c, this will uplift your business.

xxx. Insurance.

As you grow bigger, think of the business insurance, this will guarantee your business from natural disaster. So it will keep your business alive forever.

xxxi. Commerce chamber committee.

If you want to grow higher, register your business in the business chamber of commerce. I believe that every country has this kind of authoritative organ the only difference is the name used.

xxxii. Hotness.

Dear entrepreneur, remember hotness reduces work performance. There are some areas where the temperature is normally high. So if you are in such areas please plan for an air-conditioner. It will also increase your productivity.

xxxiii. Food.

Food is a very important thing to consider but be very careful because it is another area which consumes money unconsciously. Do not spend a lot of money on food especially luxurious foods. You may have money sometimes to buy expensive meals but why not eat an affordable meal? And I advise you to prefer natural foods for your brain compatibility and a healthy body.

xxxiv. Money.

Avoid being money oriented; let money be your business attachment but not your heartfelt desire. This will give you enough room of pleasure in the business field. e.g if you are in the business place and a customer comes, you exchange what you sell and the customer forgets their balance, as the customer steps away from your shop, your integrity is at a test. If you don't remind the customer, your integrity will be ruined. I also advise you dear reader; don't be afraid of engaging in loans platform. Even if you have enough money to launch a business. Your own money would not give you much discipline like borrowed money which will automatically bring discipline in financial control. Being afraid of loans means you are safeguarding yourself from free use of own money because no one will question you on the wrong use of it but borrowed money will make you think about the collaterals confiscation.

xxxv. Procrastination.

This is a business cancer that silently kills business, this is how it works; you may find a person with a good plan but keeps on moving with the following barriers:-

(a) **Feeling tired due to the number of day works**. You finally find yourself losing your focus.

(b) **Being inspired and interested in many things**, it causes the habit of postponing things especially important ones.

(c) **Priorities**: people always get confused on giving the gateway to the important things, for example: getting lunch/dinner and serving a customer. If both incidences happen in the same time, which will be given first priority? Most people give priority to things which bring out their smile, e.g "love, hobbies, popularity. They fail to prioritize tasks.

Consistence. This is a standard of dealing with internal and external forces towards your dream achievement. It is the action of unchanging standards for a long time. People do ignore opportunities by not being passionate on a particular business challenge. Remember, our body does not want to be disturbed and it always goes against the desires of our soul as we have seen before. You better stop talking about work, just make a commitment that you will do it no matter what.

CHAPTER TEN

MANAGEMENT, LEADERSHIP AND COURAGEOUS RECOGNITION AWARDS.

YEAR	EVENTS	RECOMMENDATION /AWARDS
2005	God fearing and courteous at Nyegezi Fisheries Institute Mwanza	2IC chairman of Christian Union Fisheries Fellowship (CUFF)
2006	Joined G4S with weird job achievements while upholding consent of technical seniority and by maintaining constant communication with stakeholders.	It brought no doubt to the management and became proud of outstanding company asset, whereby the senior staffs link up to a sensitive case study of fuel consumption training.
2007	A technical and professional fuel consumption and application on fuel theft crisis at Buhemba Gold Mine	Secured and saved 18,000ltrs per month valued at $27,000,000 Resulted to promotion from senior guard to section leader, plus a couple of gifts.
June 2007 to July	Transferred to Mwanza Oryx deport for venturing out grace period notice resulted from fuel theft crisis.	Arrived with technical fuel theft vulnerabilities troubleshoot, competently a year on site with no reported fuel theft incidence. Resulting promotion from section leader to inspector rank.

2008		
2008	Transferred to Geita Gold Mine as a shift supervisor in a team and commencing a new contract over there with a positive change. While at GGM, versatile, flexible, innovative and motivational tendencies were my exciting keys of responsibilities.	Resulting to site manager transfer to Buzwagi Gold Mine
2009	At Buzwagi gold mine as site manager by supporting, empowering innovative team, through:- • Regular user of Microsoft Office, including Excel, Word, PowerPoint, publisher, picture manager • Highly organized and efficient. • Excellent communication	Mesmerized customer (Barrick Buzwagi gold mine) potential customers and clients:- 1. Resulted congruent the gradual extension of contract strength from commenced 20guards to 164guards on 2011 2. Accredited member of HSE representative through mine general manager as a company. 3. Appointed to undergo security risk assessment, to PAN AFRICA mine subcontractor, persuasively done and concisely succeeded.

	skills, both written and verbal. • Polite and professional manner. • High level of attention to detail. With incredibility of uniqueness performance.	
2012	Mwadui Diamond Mine: achievement beyond borders	• Sustaining diamonds shipping from William Diamond Limited (WDL) plant to the sorting house in 5+ kilometres distance on week bases with a contingent plan.
2017	With BG /Shell, I sustained continuous improvements.	Resulted to many areas of work resumes. Finally, brought recognition via certificate award of the best controller. Later on , I was appointed to be third part time staff trainer of CCTV operator

Illustration 9:1

ABOUT THE AUTHOR

BIOGRAPHY

My name is Mr. Milton Christopher Kalwihula, a typical Tanzanian who was born on 05th July 1980 in Kagera region, Bukoba district council, in a local village known as Kitahya, located in the North-Western part of Tanzania. To-date I am 37years old. I am the firstborn in the family of eight (8) siblings from different mothers! I'm married, having one child.

My beloved late father (Julius Christopher Kalwihula) astoundingly died of a road accident on 10.07.1989, when I was 9years old. Prior to that, my father was a famous East Africa wholesaler businessman of small fish called sardines (Dagaa), and a general fish distributor. He left me at my tender age of 9years old and therefore displaced my stepmother Joyce Charles and my aunt Ester Kalwihula. Sooner than later, things started to turn around day-by-day from bad to worse. After a certain period of time, my mother cracked a smile and let all of my life independence though wasn't last. Thereafter; my mom died during deliverance at my age of 19years old, I just remember her last words "***oh! My Lord...remember and retouch my boys....!*** (*I silently said oh! Gosh...God have mercy on us*) Then she slept forever, may the lord grant her eternal life, amen. Yes! 19yrs is adulthood....but I was person from scratch, missing parental informal training and support. While a young (little boy/girl) **Lucky Dube** said: "*if they grow without a parent, who can tell them this is right and this is wrong?*" Blessed are those with either parents or a single parent. Please handle them with great care, "*when the sun goes down, stars come out*" make a serious commitment with God to make your goals come true.

Life Level One- Illness:

My life was so numeric and denominative; *"meaning that its unexplainable life"*, which always makes me drop tears flowing down my chest because of brainteasers breakthrough which resulted in earning traumatic and hurtled incidences. This was actually moral detention, which was not very easy to present or express clearly to anybody else. Even though solidifying my heart more and more; meanwhile in most cases I really failed to hold it up and wanted to give up everything around. Thinking of nobody breaking through what I am and pondering of being mistakenly born, for being scalded of....! It is when I met God presenting me (I got Jesus as Lord and my saviour).

Life Level Two-Life EXPERIMENTS and EXPERIENCE:

As much as testing deeply onto anything we might be doing (*is what we call experiments*) what gives a way to immerse deeper (*which is known as experience).* Finally, all of these gave general life awareness. The following are the vivid examples of what personally breakthrough and makes people reveal the uniqueness of life post-direction's attachment which I can say are the ones that make me being what I am today.

A firewood wholesaler and retail, charcoal-maker, cash crop cultivator like cultivating and selling sweet potatoes, as a builder (casual), carpenter, which I really mastered well up to-date; fish-monger and numerous of informal training of household activities like banana bearings, cooking food, a roistered utensils cleaner, fetching water, banana farm's weeds uprooting, washing clothes, manual hoe crops-cultivation, collecting bundle of grasses for processing banana/beans farm, from weeds, taking care of our young sisters and brothers and still need to pursue primary school education. This was differently treated when humanly mistaken, which were resulting in serious punishments once mistaking from one of above, which was actually easy to mistake.

Life Level Three-Education Status:
From primary school, I succeeded to join secondary school education, from second selection; therein was full harshness of life factors especially after the death of my mother. Special thanks go to a school teacher named Grayson Ndyetabula who acted in full response to meet necessary requirements such as giving a school plot-part for horticulture, which supported me to some extent.

As I completed my secondary school studies, life continued in both yellow and red zones. Then I thought of visiting my cousin who was living in Dodoma Thadeus Mtarubukwa and assisted what I saw was like the equivalent to who I was that time. Dodoma is the Capital city and the central part of Tanzania. My cousin introduced me to one of the famous hardware shops (FIVE STAR). Because my desire from the beginning was to see how I could advance my level of education. Two years of staying there were good enough for me to respond to this burning desire. I therefore joined Nyegezi Fisheries Institute, located in Mwanza city Tanzania for refrigeration and air-condition course whereby I however ended at the first year after failing to afford payment of college fees. Despite applying all the possible means such as requesting for the principle's recommendation letter, visiting Mwalimu Nyerere foundation, it was all in vain. I also wrote to IPP media and received no feedback and even went to specific individuals but ended up in vain.

From the very challenging situation of breakthrough, I went for informal training for fuel consumption which I mastered well, computer application course, driving school and other trainings like carpentry, CCTV Operations, Access control, IVMS course (Integrated Vehicle Movement System),

Life Level Four- Job Seeker:

With Jesus, I am proud of him, this is because being in trials for several times of serving him unsuccessfully. However, Jesus has been backing me up. As a temporary employee at by standing on his shoulder during life tragic waves whipping beyond comparison, miraculously being temporary hooked at VIC FISH INDUSTRY Mwanza as quality controller, then after joined one big security company as a security guard, where I successfully discovered my full potential.

Life Level Five -Job Careers:

When I joined a security company (**G4S**), my first appointment was in Buhemba Goldmine as security guard. My target was to collect school fees so that I could possibly continue with my studies which I really knew was what could make me meet my life's expectations. The only way was to induce covenant's diligences of *integrity, honesty, commitment and discipline*. I called these attributes God's hand upon me because through them, God gave me a fertile ground whereby senior persons, clients and outside viewers observed something different in me which led to a promotion within a month from GUARD to SENIOR SECURITY GUARD. Things moved far when I was appointed to attend the international professional team training of **fuel consumption** including computer application skills and I started gaining experience in Microsoft applications. From there, I was shifted to the fuel department and sometimes gold room security services. God offered me another gift called Passion; (*Honesty, integrity, discipline, trust-ship, passion and commitment*) which we all agree beyond doubt that no college under the sun teaches these things but being with very big dividends to the group of individual's developments. These values always remain as challenges to reach any particular person's life significances. From that task at hand, it resulted into profitable gains to the client's business market by saving 18,000liters of diesel per month equal to $27,000 by round about that time, it resulted into a double reward (gift and promotion) from SENIOR GUARD to SECTION LEADER and God added another promotion of Goodwill (*Honesty, integrity, discipline, commitment, trust-ship, passion and Goodwill*) at this point is where I started losing slowly the school mind-set and started concentrating on the job etiquettes or job careers. The company was proud of the right person in the system. Then the company had a fuel theft crisis at ORXY deport Mwanza which led to company three-month notice of contract termination and that is when I was asked and transferred to that site to regulate notice threats winning a year on site with no fuel theft incidences. For that input, another promotion from SECTION LEADER to SUPERVISOR and being transferred to Geita Gold Mine (GGM) launching a new big contract with much job-related training including safety, investigation, leadership and many more received from various resources. After one year in operation over there, being a promotional transfer to Buzwagi Gold Mine located in Shinyanga-Tanzania. Initially, a site supervisor, I operated through roles with 20 people. As far as the site grew, I was also given a rank of site manager because of adding value to my career which led to the effective business triumph and grew day by day in a number of workforces. Over there I learned a lot of helpful knowledge including *security intents, safety, ERTs, rescue from hostages, courageous causes, shift leader cause, site commander/manager course and customer care/services* and the like, and appointed to be a company HSE's mine representative, in a few months while perfecting things on the safety matters I delegated that career sharpener to another one of my team members. Three years over there, operational challenges were regulated; then I resigned, and joined another private security company (ZENETH) operating in Mwadui Diamond mine in Shinyanga-Tanzania. As a zonal commander specifically escorting Diamonds from plant to smelt-house once a week in a very successful exercise with embrace changes, while pursuing other operational attachment works. As days, months and years moved on, I looked upon my insights of computer applications; as of today, I am proud to be among the best computer application users.

Life Level Six: Fight for survival

After a promotion resulting from hard work, the battle started falling under economic interest after utilizing my faithfulness which caused fresh bullets to me. Thereafter, I was demoted with no reason but I didn't quit my job. Then I was physically given many reasons of resigning to avoid conflicting with people. I said no!!... Then the second demotion followed and still didn't give up though the harder I worked, the higher the risk. After seeing risks becoming high day by day, I started shaping another new career within the same industry (**computer application**) within 11 years of high risk of working in environments with four different companies whilst shaping computer skills. As of today, I'm living well because of being a good computer user. I really see it like a decent job for me. So I believe this is what God wanted me to be.

Life Level Seven: Rise and Fall

It also reaches a time when I get a feeling of quitting that job to follow up the internal award of entrepreneurship falling under my desire of computer application specifically in the stationery business after attending an entrepreneurship seminar from *NUEBRAND EVENT COMPANY*; for about a year in business with miserable failures. Then I thought of resuming work by winning lucrative positions in the same security industry but with a different company as contractor (Warrior/Insight security company) in BG (British Gas/Shell). This project was based in Lindi and Mtwara which are found in the Southern part of Tanzania. There was also a ranking of security dispatcher, CCTV operator and controller (*just not get confused about this please*), all of these mentioned descriptions were done under the same room with three people who were all well trained on the particular mentioned works. Therefore, no one was assigned to a specific work; it was a matter of arrangement. With BG, I successfully acquired training in IVMS (Integrated Vehicle Movement System), CCTV operator and Matrix (magnetic access control systems). I also attended a short course from Southern driving school and continuously sharpened my computer skills from Vocational Education Training Authority (**VETA**). As I write this book which I called "**Pride of Africa**", I believe in ambitious young Africans like me. I have faith in managers and leaders although there is a big problem of creating confidence on our own. The only relief is by uniting together as one. Youths have the power to change the world. From the briefly mentioned history above of my struggles, God has been good to me throughout my triumphal hustles to the extent of owning a company dealing with stationery (offices and school supply). I decided to name it "GRASS TO GRACE COMPANY LIMITED". It is not really the best but as I work harder and pray for God's assistance to enable me fulfil my dreams.

Recommendations:

The mentioned history is shows brief circumstances which have made and sharpened me to what I am today through God. I'm still working on a bigger plan and I find it valuable to share with you. It might be a gig of capacity building that may help or assist you to grab any life's golden chances. I may not have suffered more than you or I might not be well stuffed with enough data that might be needed but these are some extra things I can share with you as you may get something to learn. I say this referring to the common saying; *let the world be the classroom*. This has been a reason that drove me into collecting this information, putting it together which shows what I have experienced. Through the words of encouragement composing this text, you might be in the same track of learning something. Thank you.

BIBLIOGRAPHY

1. *Think and grow rich –Napoleon Hill*
2. *People and management-Mwl. Julius K. Nyerere*
3. *Unreachable 100 laws of business success-Brain Tracy*
4. *Challenge of Africa- Wangari Maathai @2009*
5. *Jukwaa la Sharia na Biashara – Rev. Justine Kaleb @2015 Karl Jamer Print Technology.*
6. *The covenant rights- Devid O. Oyedepo @ 2008 Dominion Publishing House (Lagos)*
7. *Natural remedies encyclopaedia*
    Author: Vence Ferrell & Harold M. Cheme published by Harstinme Book
    First Edition @1988
    Second Edition @1999
    Third Edition @2003
    Fourth Edition @2004
    Fifth Edition @2008
8. *Holy Bible @ 1997 Published jointly by Bible Society of Tanzania.*

Contacts:-

Milton C. Kalwihula.
P.O. Box 1119.
Mtwara-Tanzania.

Telephone:
+255 232 333 444

Mobile number:
+255 765 438 996
+255 688 165 838
+255 625 119 556

Email address:
miltonchristopher41@gmail.com
miltonchristopher10@yahoo.com
grasstogracecoltd@gmail.com

References

https://en.m.wikipedia.org
www.worldometers.info
www.mining-technology.com
www.encyclopedia.com
www.seriouslyfish.com